CHESHIRE

Edited by Carl Golder

First published in Great Britain in 1999 by
YOUNG WRITERS
Remus House,
Coltsfoot Drive,
Woodston,
Peterborough, PE2 9JX
Telephone (01733) 890066

HB ISBN 0 75431 530 4
SB ISBN 0 75431 531 2

FOREWORD

Young Writers have produced poetry books in conjunction with schools for over eight years; providing a platform for talented young people to shine. This year, the Celebration 2000 collection of regional anthologies were developed with the millennium in mind.

With the nation taking stock of how far we have come, and reflecting on what we want to achieve in the future, our anthologies give a vivid insight into the thoughts and experiences of the younger generation.

We were once again impressed with the quality and attention to detail of every entry received and hope you will enjoy the poems we have decided to feature in *Celebration 2000 Cheshire* for many years to come.

CONTENTS

Darnhall County Primary School

Nichola Towers	13
Claire Towers	13
Robyn Walker	14
Philip Hitchin	14
Sam Lee	15
Cherelle Champion	15
Oliver J Benjamin	16
Amanda Snelling	17
Kimberly Worrall	18
Bethany Clewes	18
Hannah Gohar	19
Amelia Berrisford	19
Katie Brittleton	19
Rachel Keep	20
Ashley Wilson	20
Kimberley Stockton	21
Thomas Woolley	21

Flowery Field County Primary School

Kate Shaw	21
Francesca Brooks	22
Sophie Connaughton	22
Kirsty Louise Gilmore	23
Bobbie Johnson	23
Razima Begum	24
Jacqui Stewart	24
Marc Kurucz	25
Erin MacDonald	26
Ashley Hesketh	26
Matthew Moss & Robin Hall-Cain	27
Kirsty Leigh	27
Catherine Stirling	28
Nicholas Balfe	28
Cara Oates	29
Michael Gratton	29
Laura Rahman	30
Brian James Porter	30

Kimberley Diane Gardner	31
Samantha Lees	31
Robert Wood	32
Ashley Dyson	32
Andrew Savill	32
Aaron Doyle	33

Greenbank School

Sophie Whittle	33
Catherine Puttick	34
Oliver Chapman	34
Matthew Williamson	35
Eleanor Page	35
Simon Peel	36
Adrian Wu	36
John Daggett	36
Jane Davies	37
Sarah Cottis	37
James Dickinson	38
Richard Rawlings	38
Charlotte Chapman	39
Jenna Wayne	39
Eleanor Mitchell	40
Rachel Sheldon	40
Andrew Totten	41
Felicity Rankin	42
Albert Suen	42
Rachael Stewart	42
David Needham	43
Edward Styles	43
Christian Bell	44
Matthew Griffin	44
Francis O'Shea Brown	45
Claire Ainley & Leanne Taylor	45
Ruaridh Guy	46
Jessica C McGeorge	47
Andrew Bennison	47
William Mitchell	48

Sara Shimi	48
Shyam Bhatt	49
Lauren King	49
Laura Spence	50
Emily Nuttall	50
Ben Styles	50
Charlotte Byrne	51
Richard Kemp	51
Alice Hess	52
Charles Fair	52
Mark Swindell	53
Laura McSorley	53
Jenna Perrin	54
Andrew Ford	54
Jon-Michael Evans	55
James Sussex	55
Elizabeth Ball	56
Sophie Bryan	56

Hare Hill School

Stacey Jones	56
Samantha Maires	57
Daniel Main	57
Rebbeca Scott	57
Adrian McBain	58
Kirsty Jones	58
Karl Whitehead	59

Hurstclough County Primary

Luke Nickerson	59
Victoria Houghton	60
Katrina Lang	60
Chelsea Merelle Cilgram	61
Lisa McCarton	61
Emma Louise Harris	62
Samuel Johnson	62
Terry John Booth	63
Rebecca Berry	63

Faye Lonergan	64
Samantha Gallagher	64
Natalie Jones	64
Michael Kelleher Moran	65
Eric Haines	65

Lower Peover CE Primary School

Vicky Barnett	66
Sarah Royle	66
Richard Roberts	67
Lisa Barbera	67
Alexander McIntyre	68
Carl Graham	68
Leanne Barlow	69
Emma Hague	69
Frances Lowe	70
Ben Washburn	71
Grace Hofton	72
David Gabbott	72
Andrew Watmore	73

Rode Heath County Primary School

Laura Boffey	73
Michelle Sigley	74
Lauren Holbrook	74
Danielle Sharples	75
Justine Bailey	75
Aimee Townley	76
Victoria Sutton	76
Heidi Banwell	77
Benjamin Woolley	77
Kathryn Williamson	78
Andrew Cain	78
Danielle Unwin	79
Hayley Baron	79
Nathan Meneghin	80
Stacey Brearley	80
Lianne Withnell	80

Jade Griffin	81
Sophie Newall	81
Amy Merrett	81

St Basil's RC Primary School, Widnes

Jennifer Batty & Katie Hodgson	82
Emma Allen	82
Daniel Bibby	83
Martin Roberts	84
Adam Prince	84
Rachael Fraser	85
April McKenna	85
Rachel Williams	86
Laura Griffiths	87
Emma Woods & Gemma Bellis	88
Aaron Rose	89
Mark Byrne & Leon Moran	90
Sarah Verity	90
Ryan Philbin	91
Emma Savage	91
Catherine Topping	92
Samantha Elwell	92
Scott Grady	93
Leah Peeney	94
John Poulson	95

Sir John Offley CP School

Kelly Adams	95
Hannah McAteer	96
Hannah Curwen	96
Laura Lightfoot	97
Amy Stonier	97

St John's CE Primary School, Sandbach

Michelle Bould	97
Lucy Hill	98
Catherine Silvester	98

The Poems

CELEBRATION 2000

Millennium Dome celebrates the new year.
The year 2000 is near.
People start to cheer.
Things that are cheap go dear.
Birds start to cheep and make a tear.
More things start to appear.

Lewis Walters (11)
Bankside Primary School

CELEBRATION 2000

The millennium is here
And people will cheer.
They celebrate the year
They have been gasping to hear.
This will occur in the new year.

Craig Vernon (11)
Bankside Primary School

SHE SITS

She sits . . . like a bird crying on a perch
She stares . . . at children walking to school
She wonders . . . if it is all going to change
She stares . . . like she is daydreaming
She prays . . . that people will say 'hiya.'

Mark Evans (10)
Castle View County Primary School

TERRIBLE TWINS

Matty and Ryan sit there sighing
until they are freed from school,
they go crazy
then calm down
and have a game of pool.

We're sure they're aliens
we're sure they're mad
but we can't really prove,
so please head teacher help us
we really need them to move.

We try to do our literacy
but they go as mad as ever
they run around crazy so much
they're probably as light as a feather.

Is anyone there to help me?
The pair are hard to tame
they have their fun
and I get the blame!

Janine Marshall (11)
Castle View County Primary School

SADNESS

She stares . . . like I'm not even here
She sits . . . like a dog waiting for a bone
She is sadder . . . that the 13th of March
When a school was destroyed by a man with a gun
She wants . . . happiness and a new boyfriend to treat her well
She prays . . . hoping that she will become a millionaire.

Aydan Jones (8)
Castle View County Primary School

THE WATER MAN

When the water man came to town
he began to dig up all the ground
I turned on the tap and the water had disappeared
what shall we do now? I feared
no water to drink
no water to wash
no water for my mum to use the mop
I sat in the chair and started to think
then I smelt a smelly stink
I looked at my feet and started to blink
thick green mist rose from my socks
pongy, whiffy, smelly, *yuk!*
I ran to the tap but got no luck
what shall I do with feet that smell like dog muck?
I sat back down with a heavy heart
thinking that me and this smell would never part
then I heard a knock on the front door
'Water's back on love' said the water man, 'puhhh!'

Sean Fell (11)
Castle View County Primary School

FISH

Fast swimming
Insect eater
Bubble blowing
Bottom dweller
Spiny backed
Sharp finned
Rainbow scaled.

Katherine Leigh (11)
Castle View County Primary School

DOG

Sharp claws
Jagged teeth
Slimy slobber
Wacky tail
Pointy ears
Spiky fur
Biscuit eater
Shoe chewer
Smelly breath
Wet nose
Mean growl.

Kimberley Wilkinson (11)
Castle View County Primary School

THE PUNCH

I was sitting down eating my lunch
When someone gave me a big punch
It knocked me flying through some metal bars
And I ended up on Mars
An alien said 'Gimme'
And I shouted 'Mummy!'
A big rocket landed on the planet that was stranded
A man got out and said 'This is a successful flight
To the Moon' and got out a spoon.

I was on the Moon!

Ivan Atanason (9)
Castle View County Primary School

FOOTBALL CRAZY

Football crazy, football crazy,
He ran round the field until he felt lazy.
Banged his head on the post,
Now he is whinging for some toast.
He is handsome and also brave,
He could do a shot that Seaman could not save.
Hit the crossie, then the post,
Then he scored and he had to boast.
It went on to pens
And lost his contact lens.
He spoofed the ball,
It ended up on the Great China Wall.
The wall fell down with all that power
And then it bounced back to the Eiffel Tower.
He got sacked and never played again,
Now he is not like any of the other men!

David Shaw (9)
Castle View County Primary School

ON A COLD COLD NIGHT

The wind blows like a torrent of darkness.
The moon sails across the ocean breeze.
The trees are stiff, the leaves have left.
The roads ride by with cars.
The stars are bright as light as a torch.
The wind roars like a lion.
It is cold and windy today, winter's coming.

Roy Chiocchi (9)
Castle View County Primary School

FISH

Bubble blowing
Worm eater
Hook swallower
Silent swimmer
Scale covered
Tail flipping
Water creature
Anglers' catch
Chip shop special
Pond dweller
Gill breather.

Amy Goodall (9)
Castle View County Primary School

MY MUM

A mum like you is what I need
To guide me through bad times
Even though you moan a bit
Your kind light is always lit
And when it's dark and cold outside
You will always be a friendly guide
And when I have bad dreams
You will always be my angel
And so when I go to bed at night
I know my mum is there in sight.

Vicky Heffey (10)
Castle View County Primary School

SHE SITS

She sits gloomily in the corner of the room
She sits with her arms folded, her face as white as a ghost
Her sleeves have been torn by her loveless husband
She has a box of tissues to wipe the tears from her face
She stares with a broken heart
But in the end it is just a play
And I am sure she is perfectly happy.

Tarrin Kennaway (9)
Castle View County Primary School

OUR HOUSE

Our house is an ark
with three dogs who often bark,
two rats who squeal and squeal
and three ferrets who chatter for their meal,
last but not least a mouse found in Karl's
bedroom in our house.

Karl Edward Avis (7)
Castle View County Primary School

SHE SITS

She sits like a bird silently in its nest
Her face tells me she needs a rest
She stares at me wherever I go
She wonders why her life has changed
She prays for God to help her
Her sadness rules her life.

Kerri Cobourne (9)
Castle View County Primary School

SHE SITS

Her life is like a pencil lead breaking every minute
She sits like a dog on a mat
She stares like a bird on its perch
She wonders when her life is to change
She prays sadly for God to help her
Her sadness rules her life
She is going slowly away and away.

Melanie Roughsedge (10)
Castle View County Primary School

SHE SANK

Her heart sank like a brick thrown in a river
Her eyelashes are as heavy as lead
A boy breaking her heart so bad
She is in a room which is never lit
She is just as sad as me and you
On a cold winter's day
When there is nothing to do.

Jessica Ayuya (9)
Castle View County Primary School

SHE SITS

She sits like a child on a wet summers day
She stares like a lion waiting for its prey
She is as bored as a person in a dark dusty room
She walks around all in the gloom
Her heart is broken
And she ends in doom.

Daniel Dunn (8)
Castle View County Primary School

A DEAD LIFE

She perched on the end of her seat like a lonely seagull on a ship
Waiting for her life to change
She is as lonely as a single grain of sand in a jar
She wishes for a miracle
Like an old apple core changing into a juicy apple
It's a dead life.

Vincent Atanasov (8)
Castle View County Primary School

SHE SITS

She sits like a lost puppy that has not been fed
She stares like a ghost that has come to haunt you
She cries like a baby waiting for its mother
Her life drifts away like smoke from a candle.

Kayleigh Francis (10)
Castle View County Primary School

SAUSAGE SUPERMAN

'Roll over' said the sausage hot from the pan,
You chips had better keep in line,
Because I'm sausage superman.

Ben Astles (8)
Church Coppenhall Junior School

HOBBIES AT HOME

Hello I'm Scott Davies and I'm eight years old,
I'll show you my hobbies new and old.
I hope you really like it, I hope you don't mind,
You can put it in Braille to be kind to the blind.

My first one is Beanie Babies
If you didn't know.
I started off in Florida
And it just went go, go, go.

My favourite ones are all of them
I just can't decide.
Some live in dark places
And some by the seaside.

If you didn't know
There's a secret I can tell.
There are new ones out for this year
There's going to be a sell.

The second one is sharks
Isn't that a surprise?
This is something boys should like
They're all quite a size.

When I watched the film *Jaws!*
I thought it was good.
That's when I got into sharks,
The Great White is not good.

Next one's a thriller
His name's Godzilla
He's ferocious and tall
Not chicken and small.

There's Robot Wars and dinosaurs
It's been nice meeting you
But here is one more hobby
I've been to see 'A Bug's Life' too!

Scott Davies (8)
Church Coppenhall Junior School

I HAVE

I have a nan
who I call gran.

I have a mum
who's quite fun.

I have a sister
who's grown a whisker.

I have a brother
who's got a lover.

I have a dad
who's not so bad.

My family is
so great
so come on
let's celebrate.

Nicola Bostock (11)
Church Coppenhall Junior School

MY FRIEND SUSIE

Susie is strong, wouldn't hurt a fly.
Susie watches bees buzzing by.
Susie has a long thin tail.
She rips up the mail.
Susie has long floppy ears and a sticky wet nose.
She kisses me with her pink slimy tongue.
Susie has a black shiny coat.
Sometimes she *pongs*.
Guess what she is?

Holly Sellars (7)
Church Coppenhall Junior School

SHARK

Pulling up the watery turf
He cuts the turquoise tide in half.
He's gnawing streamlined and glinting toothed
Pursuing his prey he stealthily moves.
This toothy arrow of the sea
Is at the peril of you and me.
Caught by hunters for their fins
What fate awaits these fearless kings?
If we don't save sharks from fishermen
There lives will come to a perilous end.

Christopher Johnson (10)
Comberbach County Primary School

THE SCREAM!

Bellowing sound
Of a scream.

Pools of colour,
Waves in the sky.

An almighty shout,
From a ghastly ghoul.

Aaaaaa!

Along the seaside shore bridge,
Boats swift and silent.

Shadows of humans,
Do they hear?

Nichola Towers (10)
Darnhall County Primary School

THE SCREAM!

The mortals walking past,
Don't seem to notice,
The alien screaming.
He stands there,
Hands over ears,
While strangers walk by,
The alien doesn't seem to notice,
He keeps screaming,
On and on and on.

Claire Towers (11)
Darnhall County Primary School

THE OLD CASTLE

There were lots of dark cellars,
They were spooky.
There had been a battle
A hundred years ago,
Everyone died.
Everyone who lived there
In the town was sad
That they lost in the battle.
The castle was bombed,
There weren't any rooms
That had survived the battle.
There were only burnt photographs,
Everything had been taken
By the people they were fighting with.

Robyn Walker (8)
Darnhall County Primary School

THE FALL OF ICARUS

Nearer, nearer I go
I fall past the stars
Past the clouds of death
Someone is shouting
'Fall Icarus fall'
'Splash' I'm in the sea
No one cares
No one helps me
I drift lower and lower
Then I fall asleep forever.

Philip Hitchin (10)
Darnhall County Primary School

THE SOWER

As I stroll through
the farmer's field
fascinated by
the lay of the crops
as the sun sets
across the landscape
I sit down and
watch the
glamorous stars
twinkle as they
lay in the black
night sky
I stay all night
to watch the sun
go down deep
and far past
the horizon.

Sam Lee (10)
Darnhall County Primary School

SINBAD THE SAILOR

Lost in the middle of nowhere
I get lonely
No one to talk to
The fish comfort me
Eat raw fish
Nothing else to eat
Salty water splashes at my face
Makes my lips sting
Sit there waiting for somebody to help me.

Cherelle Champion (11)
Darnhall County Primary School

SINBAD THE SAILOR

The sailor
In a
Boat
Coming
Close to
A giant
Wave
There
Were three
Patterned fish inside
One
Was nearly caught
By Sinbad's stick
Meant
For an oar
The other
Two fish
Looked horrified
To see
Their friend
About to go
What Sinbad didn't know
Was
That it was getting
Darker all the time.

Oliver J Benjamin (8)
Darnhall County Primary School

LANDSCAPE

I see flowers
And green grass.
I feel scared,
I try to step
Out but I can't.
I see the sun
Shining. I see
Trees and fallen
Apples. I see
Animals. I see
Some fruit,
I eat some.
I see more
Flowers.
It gets darker,
I can't see the
Sun. I hear birds
Singing. Squirrels
In the trees. I feel
Sad when I see
Fallen trees. All the
Leaves are green.
I see nests and
Drays.

Amanda Snelling (8)
Darnhall County Primary School

THE OLD CASTLE

The old castle is haunted they say,
It's falling down,
Now it's getting old,
They say the king's still there,
Searching for his wife,
The queen and the king,
Died but the king,
Came back as the ghost,
Sometimes you can see,
The king crying,
In his bedroom,
So they say.

Kimberly Worrall (11)
Darnhall County Primary School

THE OLD CASTLE

We are walking up the castle steps,
We wonder what we will see,
Cobwebs in the corner,
Spiders on the floor,
Pictures of witches,
Oooooh!
There are scary noises in the castle,
People say it's haunted by a witch,
I feel like someone's going to come and get me,
I am very, very scared.

Bethany Clewes (7)
Darnhall County Primary School

BABA YAGA AND HER FRIENDS

Witches in the forest of fears
All green, very slimy
Warts on the tip of their noses
They melt with eggs
Evil red eyes
Spiky black hair
They gurgle and mutter
Spit from holes in their faces
Remember what I said if you meet one
Scream for help or melt them with eggs.

Hannah Gohar (9)
Darnhall County Primary School

THE FALL OF ICARUS

People flying in space
Trying to grab stars as they go whizzing past.
Kids trying to turn round and round,
Trying to put your feet on the moon.

Amelia Berrisford (11)
Darnhall County Primary School

THE OLD CASTLE

We're climbing up the stairs
Don't be scared, you're not going to fall
It's only a sculpture, open the door
Go on in, look around
Find something, no do not touch that
It takes you to the dungeon!

Katie Brittleton (7)
Darnhall County Primary School

THE OLD CASTLE

There's something about it
you don't know what,
a special secret
behind the dusty bricks.
The old castle grounds
hide all evidence of life.
There's that child's rocking horse
that rocks on its own,
come in it says.
What's the secret?
We will never know.

Rachel Keep (10)
Darnhall County Primary School

BABA YAGA

Flying over towns
for a place to land
it's a full moon
pitch black night
street lights glow
in the dark
her looks make your hair stand on end
cold hands grab
you around the neck.
Help!

Ashley Wilson (10)
Darnhall County Primary School

I Am My Village

A man shouting at a lamb
On the lamb is a picture of a goat and a girl
The girl is milking the goat
People carrying stuff
A tree growing
Bright colours glowing in the dark
Little coloured homes.

Kimberley Stockton (8)
Darnhall County Primary School

The Fall Of Icarus

Someone floating on water
Someone falling out of the sky
Someone floating in space
A shadow of someone.

Thomas Woolley (7)
Darnhall County Primary School

Candle

Candle, candle flickering, glittering in the night,
A candle in the night orange illuminating light,
Never touch the golden yellow flame,
Dampen the light to let it glimmer,
Light glow, light gloom,
Every night let your light shimmer.

Kate Shaw (9)
Flowery Field County Primary School

SPELLS

Slugs, snails, fleas and worms,
All mixed up as filthy germs,
Frogs' legs and cows' eyes,
Made to look like mince pies,
Baby birds and baby chicks,
Little stones and dirty sticks.
The witches stir their evil brew,
A pie for me and a pie for you.
Tempting smiles they lure their prey
To take the gift of life away,
Old and weary, toothless grin,
Take my breath a brand new pin.
First the slugs and then the worms,
Snails, fleas and smelly germs,
Froggy legs and cows' big eyes,
Leaping from the tasty pies.
Baby birds and baby chicks,
All the stones and dirty sticks,
But fear you well this bad disguise,
Don't ever eat the witches' pies.

Francesca Brooks (11)
Flowery Field County Primary School

SPRING'S DAFFODILS

Spring's daffodils, spring's daffodils,
Dancing all around you,
Children picking the wonderful daffodils,
They put spring into your heart to see the lovely daffodils,
They're just like bright yellow buttercups with beautiful
golden trumpets put inside them,
I love to see spring's daffodils.

Sophie Connaughton (8)
Flowery Field County Primary School

OUT IN ALL WEATHERS

It snowed in the night,
And the whole world is white.
I'm off out with my friends,
For a mighty snow fight.

It's windy today
And the trees swing and sway.
See the wind take my kite,
Up, up, up and away.

Today it's all rain,
It's really a pain.
I could just stay in,
And watch telly again,
But maybe not yet,
Instead I'll just get
My wellies and things
And go out and get wet.

Kirsty Louise Gilmore (9)
Flowery Field County Primary School

YELLOW

The sun is like a yellowy golden
fire ball passing through the air.

A daffodil stands proudly in the fields
standing out like the sun, petals like rays.

The sandy, shining beach is burning
from the sun.

Sunflowers are wildly coloured yellow, bright
and beautiful.

Bobbie Johnson (11)
Flowery Field County Primary School

WINTER

Hush!
It is the wintry night-time
In the small town,
The snow is pieces of white round paper
Falling from the sky.
Children and parents are snuggled in their beds
Like peaceful angels.
Animals are hibernating now
Praying for the cold winter to go away.
The fires of the houses are crackling
Burning red-hot,
The owls are hooting and screeching
Like angry dogs barking for their food,
The cosy houses are sleeping silently
The wind is howling loudly,
Like a fierce tiger growling for its prey,
Colourful leaves land lightly on the ground.
It is winter!

Razima Begum (11)
Flowery Field County Primary School

YELLOW

Yellow, like the bright, hot sunlight at noon.
Yellow, like the chicks, sunflowers, daffodils
like golden rays of sunlight.
Yellow, a happy, bold, bright, beautiful colour,
Fiery from the golden sun.
Yellow, the corn in a field in the countryside.
Yellow, the sign of new life and happiness.

Jacqui Stewart (10)
Flowery Field County Primary School

SPRING

Spring brings flowers,
a colourful sight,
dancing around in the
bright sun light.
It makes me feel
happy and gay, on
a beautiful sunny day.

Spring, with the breeze
rustling the trees,
lambs skipping to and fro.
Children playing happily
with their friends,
wishing this season would
never end.

After spring comes the
summer days,
when we all have our
holidays.
Down at the seaside
having fun,
laughing and playing
everyone.

Marc Kurucz (8)
Flowery Field County Primary School

JACK FROST

You cannot see sight of him
Look there he is all very light
My eyes are hurting very bad
Hush!
He is silent, he is quiet
Don't go near him
Oh no, he is coming near us
He is silent, he is quiet again
He is coming closer
He looks like a very light blue
He has sharp fingers like icicles
He makes the air look frosty
He has to go now
He has gone now.

Erin MacDonald (10)
Flowery Field County Primary School

THE DAFFODIL

It stands up straight like a soldier,
Keeping an eye on the lawn.
Its beautiful colours protect it from evil creatures.

The leaves are its defence
Just in case anything comes through
And even if it does . . .
It won't last long.

The daffodil, the daffodil
It is so beautiful.
The daffodil, the daffodil,
It is so wonderful.

Ashley Hesketh (11)
Flowery Field County Primary School

MUM

My mum is great, my mum is smart,
In my house she plays her part,
she cleans and cooks
and tidies my books,
that's how great my mum is.

She doesn't fuss in my room,
she just keeps sweeping with her broom,
after she cooks she doesn't rest,
this is because she is the best,
that's how great my mum is.

She makes my tea, she makes me a drink
when I'm doing my homework and I can't think.
My mum is always there to help me on my way,
That's how great my mum is.

Matthew Moss & Robin Hall-Cain (11)
Flowery Field County Primary School

WINTER

It is a winter moonless night,
The wind is roaring,
The rain is like water coming out of your tap,

      Hush!

Leaves are falling off trees,
And the bare trees shiver.
All the colour fades away,
Freeze, freeze the winter sky,
Then high-ho! The holly!
Life is so jolly.

Kirsty Leigh (10)
Flowery Field County Primary School

SPLINTERING WINTER

The soft snow is white flour,
The village is silent,
No one is in a rush,
So hush!
A snowman is as tall as a big round tower.
You can see all the children having snowball fights,
But when ice gets on the hills, the wind starts to bite
And the snow is dripping and dropping swiftly down.
The fog is once again swirling in and out of the frosty town.
The ground is filling up with snow,
You can almost feel the ice on the tip of your toe.
You can smell the morning's fresh air,
When the trees are brown and bare.
Everything is covered with snow, even the trees,
And the ground is piled with dead leaves.
And now the whole countryside is chilled,
With children's happy faces with grins and thrills.

Catherine Stirling (11)
Flowery Field County Primary School

WILL THERE BE A WINTER?

Will there be a winter in the year 2000?
Will we have a winter at all?
Will the trees still be bare?
Will we get the fun out of winter?
Will our mums still be paying the gas bill
because the fire's on full?
Will the beggars be having fun or will they
be like snowmen on a frosty day?

Nicholas Balfe (11)
Flowery Field County Primary School

WINTER POEM

The black choking smoke swirls through the sky,
And the wailing wind,
Listen!
You can hear crackling of flames,
And the snow softly bouncing on the ground,
But, there I see in the darkness,
A dog shivering in the wilderness,
Like a twirling cyclone,
I can feel the frosty air biting at me,
As I look up into the air,
I see no stars,
Nor any moon,
For all I see is a black bandaged night,
I can just see the snowy hills,
And the taste of the charcoal smoke,
Slowly falling to sleep.

Cara Oates (10)
Flowery Field County Primary School

IMAGINE A . . .

Imagine a fish as fat as a dish,
Imagine a cat as small as a rat,
Imagine a pig as thin as a twig,
Imagine a dog as long as a log,
Imagine a croc as fat as a rock,
Imagine a snail as tall as a sail,
Imagine a toad as black as a road,
Imagine a school as clean as a pool,
Imagine this end as tight as a bend.

Michael Gratton (11)
Flowery Field County Primary School

HUNGER

Please do not throw away the food crumbs
you cannot eat.
For many a starving child will find
it a treat.

Chips, crisps, a sausage or two in our tummy
such a delight.
But for the poor they go to bed
hungry at night.

We should not waste
food that is put on our plate.

We must always know how it feels
when hunger shatters people's dreams.

Laura Rahman (10)
Flowery Field County Primary School

WINTER

Hush
Listen to the soft snow falling
Can you see it?
It is covering everything on the snowy hills
The rough sea, the darkness
But most of all, winter.
It's the moonless night,
Icicles hang from the branches
Of trees like white bats.

Brian James Porter (11)
Flowery Field County Primary School

A WINTER NIGHT

The lost dog shivered in the frozen wilderness
like an anthracite statue hidden away in shadows.
Everything was still.
You could hear the trees swaying in the wind.
The hailstones were like a huge box of marbles being
tipped upon a model village.
The town was still on the Earth.
The untrodden snow lay flat on the ground
like white wool stuck together.
Hush!
The wind was swirling around the chimney pots and whistling.
Everybody in the town was sleeping.

Kimberley Diane Gardner (11)
Flowery Field County Primary School

JACK FROST

Jack Frost is a person you're not like,
He makes everything frosted,
He's a cruel person you won't like,
He makes the air fresh,
But he makes it cold too,
Through the lakes he goes,
And everything froze,
And as morning comes,
He dies.

Samantha Lees (10)
Flowery Field County Primary School

JACK FROST

Who is the one who ices the houses?
Jack Frost is the one
The one who puts the icicles upon the frozen trees
The dumbfounded town does not know
That Jack Frost has put ice upon everyone
Jack Frost left the town in whiteness
But the town does not know
That Jack Frost has been and gone.

Robert Wood (10)
Flowery Field County Primary School

WINTER FIELDS

Hush!
The dumb found fields,
Frozen like the dead,
The black bandaged night wraps up the Earth,
You can almost hear the silent sounds of the wind,
You see the frozen sky drifting among the clouds.

Ashley Dyson (10)
Flowery Field County Primary School

THE CROCACAT

A head like a snake, a neck like a drake.
A back like a beam, a belly like a bream.
A foot like a cat, a tail like a rat.
A leg like a twig, an arm like a pig.
Ears like sails, eyes like snails.
A mouth like a croc, a tooth like a rock.

Andrew Savill (10)
Flowery Field County Primary School

CAMPING IN WINTER

From far away,
The tent looks like a seagull,
Breathing in the frosty air,
Makes you shiver,
When you get up in the morning,
You have icicles on your nose,
Throbbing fingers,
Red toes.

Aaron Doyle (10)
Flowery Field County Primary School

THE BEE

Bzzz!
Softly, silently, secretly,
the bee guards his prey,
making sure his pollen is safely
guarded all the day.

Staring at the blazing sun,
like fire it gleams in the night
it shines and sparkles
in the moon of the night.

A bird cheeps, a little groan,
the slightest noise and the bee wakes up.
Slowly he flies
softly to the flower cup.

He slowly likes
the descending yellow;
then he flies back
to the mellow moonlight.

Sophie Whittle (10)
Greenbank School

FLUTTER BY

The butterfly farm is always full, butterflies flit everywhere,
Time and time again they flutter by,
Flutter by butterfly,
Time to stop for a drink by the fountain,
Have a sip of nectar,
Flutter by butterfly,
Rest on a shady palm leaf,
Fly up to the glass roof to stretch in the sunlight,
Flutter by butterfly,
The butterfly tries to flit away from children too close to him,
They want to hold him, squeeze him,
The children are called by their mother, the butterfly is
Left in peace with his fellow butterflies,
The sun goes down, the moon comes up,
The butterfly drifts off to sleep.

Catherine Puttick (10)
Greenbank School

SEA

The white horses crashing against the cliffs.
The lighthouse alerting the sailing ships.
The fishing ships come out and
Throw out their big nets.
As they haul in their nets,
They open them and out falls
A big pile of sparkling fish.
They gather them up,
And put them in boxes.
They would sail back to the shore.

Oliver Chapman (10)
Greenbank School

KOALA

The koala jumps up the bark of a tree,
Scratch,
Scratch,
Go his toes,
Higher and higher the koala goes.

Higher and higher, he's nearly there,
Shake,
Shake,
Goes his black hair.

Then, at last, he reaches the top,
And leans over,
As if to drop.

His large eyes are looking at me,
He's staring down from the eucalyptus tree.

Then he runs off,
Leaving his spot,
And runs and runs, until all you can see is a tiny dot.

Matthew Williamson (9)
Greenbank School

THE BEAST

I'm mean and I'm keen for my food,
And if you don't I'll be in a mood,
Maybe some ham or maybe a ram,
I don't care, for I'm a bear,
I may be nasty, so don't be hasty
When I eat you, you'll be tasty.

Eleanor Page (9)
Greenbank School

WINTER AS A SQUIRREL

I go around collecting nuts to hibernate
It all goes very cold
All the kids get wrapped up tight
Go inside all warm
All the trees are bare
I jump from branch to branch
But no leaves are there
It all goes dark.

Simon Peel (9)
Greenbank School

ELEPHANT

I walk and walk and walk
But I never stop. That's because I am an
Elephant, waiting for a water hole.
It is quite hard but I think it's worth it, do you?
We are rare African elephants
And you can keep your guns away
Because we are endangered,
Go away because we'll stay.

Adrian Wu (10)
Greenbank School

RED

Red can be lots of things
Apples, letter boxes, those kind of things.
Apples are red, juicy and crunchy.
Leaves in autumn, red as can be,
My brother goes red when he is angry at me.

John Daggett (9)
Greenbank School

THE SEA'S EMOTIONS

The sea has two sides,
One on each tide.
The first crashing,
Among the rocks and bashing
From place to place,
With lots of haste.
The second being onto the shore foam,
With sea creatures' little homes.
The sea gently twists,
This time with no hiss.
It often twirls,
Or maybe even whirls.
Above it all is the glorious blue sky,
In it lies the beautiful golden sun,
Shining whatever mood the sea is in!

Jane Davies (11)
Greenbank School

CAMELS

Camels are sometimes called 'Ships of the Desert'
Stored in their humps is fat to live off.
They carry people and goods.
There are four different species of camel,
All with wide splayed feet.
They live in the deserts.
The Bactrian camel of Central Asia
And the larger Dromedary of the Middle East
Gangly legs, humped body, a long broad neck.
They look as if they have been made up
From the parts of half a dozen animals.

Sarah Cottis (8)
Greenbank School

AUTUMN

In autumn the leaves
Are brown, red, yellow and orange
November rockets zooming
Catherine wheels spinning
Guy Fawkes burning red and hot
Hallowe'en witches zooming
Vampires too
Witches cackling
Ho'oooo
Autumn trees are bare
Foxes hunting
Owls hooting
Sparrows beware
Squirrels storing nuts
Bees making honey
Wasps galore.

James Dickinson (9)
Greenbank School

CHIMPANZEE

C limbing trees and falling off,
H ome for him is the rainforest.
I   n his tree with his family,
M eals he eats like you and me.
P   laying happily in the sun,
A   ll the chimps have lots of fun.
N ear the river where they drink,
Z   oos are where you see them.
E   ating lots of different foods,
E   ven bugs and insects too.

Richard Rawlings (10)
Greenbank School

WHO AM I?

There are two types of us
We stamp around the jungle
With trees on either hand
And make the Earth core rumble
The lions begin to roar
I have a snake, not too big
It sucks up leaves and twigs
And never ever ever stops
Putting them inside me
I have big ears
They keep me cool
On either hand of my snake
I have sharp and pointed things
Which help me fight for my tea.

Charlotte Chapman (9)
Greenbank School

THE HUNTER

Snap! There he goes again,
Eating any tasty morsel that swims too near;
Too near for the crocodile,
His squinting eyes disappear;
Something gleaming in the water; he surfaces,
Swerving - shimmering - streaming down the river,
He turns, his small eyes see something interesting,
The crocodile darts back, nothing, nothing he snivels;
Down he goes into the murky depths of the river,
Nothing else good to eat;
His razor sharp teeth show and disappear again;
He then paddles home to rest, ready for tomorrow's hunt.

Jenna Wayne (10)
Greenbank School

THE SEA

Lapping waves touch the shingle,
Reaching for the sand.
I feel the foam beneath my feet,
And rock beneath my hand.

Blue and green the sea shines,
Shells of many hues.
Sailing high upon the wind,
A lone seagull mews.

Then the sky darkens,
A white crest foams.
Raging about the sea,
Pearly horses roam.

Under the sea is blissful calm,
Fish lazily swim.
A shark chases hungrily,
Jaw onto fin.

In the barren world,
A lighthouse stands.
Crashing waves it disperses,
A beacon to ships that land.

Eleanor Mitchell (10)
Greenbank School

THE DOLPHIN

The dolphin's silver streak glistens in the sunset,
Whilst he glides around the seabed,
He leaps and sails through the air,
Before diving down for food.

The dolphin eats fish and seaweed for supper,
He devours them with care,
Then, he dives for the last time and takes a long, deep breath,
Before settling down to sleep.

Rachel Sheldon (9)
Greenbank School

THE TRUE TERROR OF THE SEAS

Scary, murderous sharks with
their cruel sharp teeth,
are they the terror of the seas?
No.
Poisonous frightening fish with
their sharp pointed spines,
are they the terror of the seas?
No.
Scythe-like swordfish with their
long lances,
are they the terror of the seas?
No.
Slippery sea snakes with their
deadly bite,
are they the terror of the seas?
No.
The true terror of the seas,
my friends spill oil, crumble coral,
hunt the rare . . .

They are . . . humans.

Andrew Totten (12)
Greenbank School

THE CAMEL

The camel is hot and bothered with no water for miles around.
It slowly plods on and on dragging his weary feet, weak and tired.
The sun is blazing down on him,
second after second, minute after minute,
day after day, week after week.
Slowly walking on, stepping carefully.
People all around just staring but giving no water
to the thirsty camel to quench his thirst,
wondering whether he would find an oasis . . .
But the camel never gave up.

Felicity Rankin (10)
Greenbank School

CAT

The cat is humbly sleeping in her basket.
The cat is lifting herself,
On her four long, stiff legs.
She yawns and pads away,
With her long tail tucked away.

Albert Suen (9)
Greenbank School

THE SEASIDE

The lapping sea against the rocks,
and the multicoloured shells,
dotted along the seaside,
the sea, a deep dark blue,
and the scorching hot sand
burns my feet.

The rock pool , though bursting with life
is as still as a mill pond.
The animals in the rock pool
are so beautifully coloured.
The crab goes to the snail.

Rachael Stewart (11)
Greenbank School

THE SEA

Deep down at the bottom of the sea lies the shipwreck,
Smothered with coral reef as it lies there motionless.
The sand sinking into the gaps in the wood.
Colourful fish glistening in the sun and the sea horses
Rolling round as the gentle waves pushed towards the shore.
I could hear the distant squeals of the dolphins as they draw closer.
Walking along the beach shore,
I heard the crunch of the shells beneath my feet.
I picked one up and listened to the sound of the sea.

David Needham (11)
Greenbank School

TEETH

My teacher's teeth are the weirdest teeth I have seen
They are big, yellow and horrid
But my grandad's teeth are the weirdest teeth
When I sleep over
They stare at me in a little jar
I always wonder whether he has teeth.

Edward Styles (9)
Greenbank School

SNAKE!

                        The
                    snake
                squiggles
            on
            the
            sand
        its
        tongue
            a-
                flickering
                It
                    sees
                        a
                        rat
                            and
                                swallows
                            like
                        a
                    cat.

Christian Bell (9)
Greenbank School

THE DOG

Woof woof woof, I keep you up all night,
Bark bark bark, I give the cats a fright.
I am the dog, man's best friend,
Our friendship will never come to an end.
I bring him the paper and the mail,
And when I'm bored, I chase my tail.
I sleep softly at my master's feet,
And when I'm good I get a treat.

Matthew Griffin
Greenbank School

SPIDER IN THE BATHTUB

'Bath time Jim'
Mum said to him
I'm really the best
Off went the vest.

On went the hat
In came Pat
Turn on the water
Then I saw her!
The spider!

It was hairy
And it was scary
Get the hammer
Before it scuttles
Across the floor.

'Kill it Jim'
Mum said to him
I'm really the best
On went the vest.

Francis O'Shea Brown (10)
Greenbank School

CAT

A small domesticated furry creature.
She *purrs* like a lawnmower.
Miaow - she's a playful cat, and then she leaps on my lap
with a great gigantic crocodile yawn.
Then *flash,* she's asleep, and as quiet as a mouse for the rest of the day.

Purr, purr, purr.

Claire Ainley (9) & Leanne Taylor (10)
Greenbank School

SEA ANIMALS

The sea,
Most of the world's surface,
Three quarters of the Earth's surface,
All of it teaming with life,
From the smallest plankton,
To the hugest whale.
Every cubic centimetre,
Full of wondrous creatures.
Lobsters, pike, salmon and halibut,
Minnows, dolphins, whales, deadly sharks.
Sea urchin spike the unsuspecting swimmer,
Painful but not deadly.
Another swimmer is not so lucky,
His encounter with the sea snake,
In the warm waters of Australia proves fatal.

Some animals are friendly,
Some are not.
Some are poisonous,
Some are not,
Some are colourful,
Some are not.
All are wonderful,
Some live down in the deep depths,
Some live in shallow rock pools.

All these animals are unique,
All are fantastic,
All are under threat,
Under threat by mankind.

Ruaridh Guy (10)
Greenbank School

WINTER

No green on the trees,
Summer has gone to bed,
Winter is ready,
To spring up your nose,
Sometimes weather is bad.

Winter colours brown and white,
Frost so hard,
Will it snow?
Yes, I don't know,
Will it ever let go?

Trees are being cut down,
For people to decorate,
Animals hibernating,
Birds flying away.

Sky gets dark at 5 o'clock,
Let's turn on the light,
When it's night-time and the moon is up,
Children are asleep all nice and snug.

Jessica C McGeorge (8)
Greenbank School

THE RAPTOR

The raptor is fast and cunning,
If you see one you better start running.
But when you run it won't
Be fun;
His thick legs will pounce
On you!
Oh dear, that's the end of you.

Andrew Bennison (9)
Greenbank School

BLUE

Blue is a wonderful colour
Black is just a lot duller
Sky shining in the air
Sapphires glowing everywhere
Violets fragrant as can be
The fish swimming in the blue sea
The moon shining in the sky
Eagles hunting with their sharp blue eyes
Marbles rolling on the ground
Blue tits sing making a sound
Blue coral on the sea bed
Sweden's flag flying proud
In the blue sky passes a cloud
Blue is a wonderful colour
Black is just a lot duller.

William Mitchell (9)
Greenbank School

YELLOW

Sun makes me happy, it makes me hot and thirsty too!
Leaves in autumn dropping silently,
Bright yellow, happy as can be,
Dusters shining, polishing away,
Bright yellow makes everything glow.
Yellow is a happy colour,
Makes everything stand out.
Sunflowers and wheat in a cornfield,
While bees and wasps buzz around.
Sand in the deserts,
Camels plodding along.

Sara Shimi (8)
Greenbank School

RED

Poppies are red
Apples red and juicy
Love is red
Rubies have beauty
Manchester United
Our best team
Red's nothing like green
Roses are red
Scented and fragrant
Pretty, beautiful
Petals soft as silk
Red sunset over the sea
Red is not hard to see
Red is a colour I like to see
Red is as beautiful as can be
Red is for love
That is sometimes said
Red you can think about
When you are in bed.

Shyam Bhatt (9)
Greenbank School

RED

Red is for poppies all in the field
Red is robin red breast
Red is hot on a summer's day
Rubies are red, all shiny and bright
Lots of leaves are red, all crunched up and old
Red roses on a summer's day
Red new mountain bike, clean as can be
Red apples fresh from the tree, tasty and crunchy, ready for me.

Lauren King (8)
Greenbank School

Rock Pool

Looking in the rock pool,
It is full of life.
Starfish, sprats and sea horses,
All living without strife,
Green seaweed waving in the chill water,
Crabs scuttling over pebbles and sand,
Disappear to a far off land,
Jellyfish float, limpets stick,
Fishes swim in the deep,
While the hermit crab gets some sleep.

Laura Spence (11)
Greenbank School

The Sea

The waves crashing on the shore.
The sea roars whilst lapping on the shore.
The golden sand between your feet.
Seashells twist into all different shapes and sizes.
The pinkie hue of the coral on the sea bed.

The golden sun beams on the beautiful blue sea
The dolphins jump and come.

Emily Nuttall (11)
Greenbank School

Seashore

Children playing in the sand,
Grown-ups listening to the seashore band.
Everyone's swimming in the sea,
Eating ice-creams one, two and three.

Waves crashing on the sand,
People skimming stones, across the big blue land.
Fishes swimming everywhere,
A school of whales bobbing up here and there.

Ben Styles (11)
Greenbank School

YELLOW

Buttercups are yellow, there are hundreds in that field.
They're gold and a quite bright yellow.
Sunshine is bright yellow-red, it lights up the sky and makes it warm.
Hay, hay lives in a field of harvest mice.
My English book is yellow, a dull warm yellow and I sort of like it.
Stars are shiny, hard and bright, I think they're like a lock of light that
Stays all night and goes in the morning, they're wonderful little things.
Dry grass is funny, it's crunchy and delicate, it's blunt and rough
As well and doesn't have anything inside.
My brother has a bedroom that is bright, warm and yellow all over.

Charlotte Byrne (8)
Greenbank School

RAINBOW POEM

Red fire sweeps through the forest burning the trees
Orange sky as the sun is setting
Yellow is the sun in the sky
Green is the grass and the leaves of the trees
Blue is the sky with the clouds floating
Indigo is the sea swiftly crashing on the shore
Violet is the cloak made for a king.

Richard Kemp (9)
Greenbank School

WINTER

Cold frost bites on my face and hands
When in the mornings I'm late for school
Sitting in the car as bored as can be
Wait for the car to get its act together
And de-ice itself
When I get to school I have a snowball fight with my friends
And come in soaking wet
I dry myself off and go into class.

For winter so cold and wet
Winter means snowflakes dropping on my head
All the squirrels and hedgehogs are in hibernation
The leaves go crunch when we walk around
Ice frosts on windowpanes.

Alice Hess (8)
Greenbank School

AUTUMN

Autumn cold, woolly jumpers
Children cold, heaters on
Socks up, long sleeves,
Summer over, sun gone,
Colder nights, rockets fly across the sky,
Bang, bomb, swish, wish,
Hallowe'en witches and goblins,
Lots of children, lots of sweets,
Hard conkers, shiny too,
Hungry squirrels, storing nuts,
Climbing trees, knocking conkers on the floor,
Back to school, different teachers, different class,
This is autumn.

Charles Fair (8)
Greenbank School

THE SWIFT CHEETAH

It runs with the sand,
Crumpling beneath its furry feet,
Searching for its prey,
He runs even further,
Out on the African Plain,
He spots a hunter,
Runs to the grass,
He camouflages there,
He waits, the hunter passes by,
He waits until he can pounce,
The hunter gets too shocked to shoot,
The cheetah triumphs again.
I hope this story tells you,
The cheetah's too swift to test.

Mark Swindell (9)
Greenbank School

THE FOX

Silent through the night
Looking for its prey
A long body, a wet nose
And a bushy tail creeping around.

In the morning bright and shiny
The creature slowly creeps away
Through the day the mother gives birth
To a single cub.

The mother is very happy
As it sleeps away.

Laura McSorley (9)
Greenbank School

THE ADDER

Slither through the night,
Trying with might,
To find mice and birds,
The enemies are near like eagles,
The adder, green and black,
Hissing at whatever it sees,
Spit out its tongue and got it!
It's a mouse pleading for its life,
The adder just hisses,
And lets it go,
Goes back home to the group,
And has a sleep,
Having nothing to eat.

Jenna Perrin (8)
Greenbank School

THE RHINO

Grey is the colour
Tough is the skin
Sharp are the horns
Big and fat
Sharp are the nails
Hiding in the mud
There goes a human
And . . .
It springs out and charges
The human gets his gun ready
Wham!
The rhino has got him.

Andrew Ford (8)
Greenbank School

THE ROCK POOL

In the rock pool
Freezing cold water
Crabs and lobsters lurking around
Be careful they might nip you.

In the rock pool
Slippery are the rocks
Don't bang your head
Or you will ruin your holiday.

In the rock pool
Don't tease the crabs
Or you will end up crying
And you will have to go home.

Jon-Michael Evans (10)
Greenbank School

THE SEA

The golden hot sand
The blue sky and sparkling shells
That glisten in the sun's reflection
Shells, all shapes and sizes
Colours and textures
Red, blue, orange and green
The roaring sea
Blue and green
All the sea creatures
Slithering and gliding through the water
A truly beautiful experience.

James Sussex (11)
Greenbank School

RAINBOW POEM

Red roses you see them all around.
Orange when you get a sunset.
Yellow, the sun when it's a pleasant day.
Green grass you walk on.
Blue is the sea at the seaside.
Indigo is the dark sky at the night.
Violet after a storm has been.

Elizabeth Ball (9)
Greenbank School

THE SNAKE

The slinky, slanky snake slithers slowly, slyly, softly
Round and round upon the ground.
Slithering, silkily, silently, silently without a sound.
His pattern goes slowly, slowly away he goes.

Sophie Bryan (9)
Greenbank School

FLOWER!

Nodding, sighing
Bobbing flower
Juicy pollen
Whispering flower
Growing, swaying
Graceful flower
Fresh, colourful
Glowing flower.

Stacey Jones (10)
Hare Hill School

CANDLE

Smooth, dry, round and stiff,
Standing like a candlestick.
Hiss that blows smoke so high,
Sizzles that scratch like a curled up candle.
Yellow flame that's glowing bright,
Dancing gently, hot and bright.
Purple, white, yellow and blue,
All the colours the candle has.

Samantha Maires (8)
Hare Hill School

CANDLE

Dry, round, white candle
Pointing, stiffly, solid wax
With a scrape and sizzle
With a burning smell that
Sends smoke into the air
Shining, glowing, melting wax
Dancing, slowly, yellow flame
Swaying gently like a flower.

Daniel Main (10)
Hare Hill School

KITTEN

Giddy, sweet like kitten
Colourful, flashy eyes.

Quick, playful, fluffy kitten
Clean, smooth, black and white kitten
Beautiful, smart, clever kitten.

Rebbeca Scott (9)
Hare Hill School

WAVES

Tossing, crashing, splashing waves
Rapid, racing, monstrous waves
Crashing, sizzling, lashing, killer waves.

Waves, waves, waves.

Fast, gentle, calm waves.
Quiet, silent, soundless waves
Smooth, tender, flat waves
Blue, dark, white waves
Beautiful, pretty, cold waves.

Waves ,waves, waves.

Adrian McBain (10)
Hare Hill School

CANDLE

Dull, smooth, dry candle,
solid wax, pointing wick.

Sizzle, scrap, hiss of black smoke,
curled in a candle.

White glowing flame,
dancing gently, purple base.

Transparent yellow flame, swaying,
hot and hazy.

Kirsty Jones (8)
Hare Hill School

BIRD

Swooping, flapping,
Whooping, soft, sweet
Feathers.
Flapping, soft, whooping
Birds.
Soft, sweet, swooping
Birds.
Furry, floppy, white birds.
Hovering, sweet birds.

Karl Whitehead (9)
Hare Hill School

A POEM ON THE MILLENNIUM

I was on the moon
and it went so soon.

It came so soon
with a big boom.

The millennium came
with a big kaboom!
and a broom came across
the room.

The parties started
the music boomed.

The parties silenced
the music stopped
it all went quiet
then went *riot.*

Luke Nickerson (11)
Hurstclough County Primary

THE MILLENNIUM

The millennium comes every
Thousand years
When the fireworks go off
Everyone cheers.

In the year two thousand
Will all the computers blow up?
Or will Manchester United
Win the European Cup?

The answer to these
Only time will tell
But when Big Ben strikes
I'll be giving out a big yell.

I'm glad to be around for this
Very special time
When people will have celebrations
And drink lots of wine.

Victoria Houghton (10)
Hurstclough County Primary

MILLENNIUM BUG

Millennium Bug
don't lie on the rug
or you'll catch the Millennium Bug

Don't cuddle up with the bear
don't sit on the chair
because the Millennium
Bug's been there.

Katrina Lang (10)
Hurstclough County Primary

CELEBRATION 2000

The millennium is here
Let's go out and cheer
Let's go and have some beer
The millennium is here.

The millennium is here
They all cheer
The men get some beer
The millennium is here.

The millennium is here
The men go mad on beer
They cheer and there's beer
The millennium is here.

The millennium is ending
Let's go home and end it.

Chelsea Merelle Cilgram (9)
Hurstclough County Primary

MILLENNIUM POEM

The Millennium Bug is nearly here,
It comes upon us every thousand years,
The children will be dancing,
Their parents will be prancing,
Fireworks will be banging,
Oh what fun we'll be having,
People will be jumping around and around,
And children will make a loud sound!

Lisa McCarton (9)
Hurstclough County Primary

CELEBRATION 2000

In the year 2000
It's gonna be
Fabulous, excellent
And wicked.

It's gonna be
Great, fantastic
And lovely
In the year 2000.

In the year 2000
It's gonna be
Glamorous, beautiful
And marvellous.

It's gonna be a
Day to remember.

Emma Louise Harris (9)
Hurstclough County Primary

MILLENNIUM

M illennium is not far away. Where will
I   be on that great day?
L   aughing and joking with the rest. Will these bugs
L   ive up to the test?
E   ach one causing trouble where it can
N   o electricity to use the fan
N   o gas to light the pan. Where will
I   be on that great day?
U   nder mum's feet? I cannot say
M   illennium is not far away.

Samuel Johnson (9)
Hurstclough County Primary

MIDNIGHT

Watch out this year, beware
The clock's about to strike twelve
Hooray, hooray, it's here at last
Children will be dancing with joy
Families will be prancing like mad
Babies will be sleeping
Fireworks will be exploding
Children will be shouting hooray
Fires will be lit with burning flames
Sparklers will be put in buckets
What a happy millennium this year.

Terry John Booth (8)
Hurstclough County Primary

THE MILLENNIUM PARTY

Millennium 2000
In the time when it has come
You will see everyone celebrating
All because of this special year
The year 2000, so when it has come
There will be lots of people having parties
And putting balloons up for the party
Even they will play on their PCs, the 2000 kind
So that is what will happen in the year
2000!

Rebecca Berry (11)
Hurstclough County Primary

MILLENNIUM

Fireworks, fireworks
Little Mrs Moon in the sky
Fireworks, fireworks in the sky
Rock-a-bye-bye
Year 2000 celebration is coming near
If we report it to the news the whole land will hear
When is it coming, the happiness day?
Let the horses have some hay
Don't forget, let them say neigh, neigh.

Faye Lonergan (8)
Hurstclough County Primary

YEAR 2000

Y   ear two thousand
E   choes of the past
A   ll the people cheering, oh what a sound
R   ight across the land
2   thousand years have passed
O   ff go the fireworks up in the sky so bright
O   h what a sight
O   n and on for another 2000 years.

Samantha Gallagher (8)
Hurstclough County Primary

CELEBRATION 2000

Happy New Year is the cry,
2000 years has just gone by.
War and famine, disease and drought,
Why can't we have peace throughout?

Happy New Year is the cry,
2000 years have just gone by.
War and famine, disease and drought,
Why can't we have peace throughout?

Natalie Jones (9)
Hurstclough County Primary

THE YEAR 2000

Fireworks will bang
Balloons will go up
Computers beware of the Millennium Bug
At the start of the year 2000
Celebrations and parties will begin
The Millennium Dome will let everybody in
On the 1st of January everybody will see
It's the start of a new century
My mum, dad, sister and me!

Michael Kelleher Moran (8)
Hurstclough County Primary

CELEBRATION 2000

Raise a glass and give a cheer
The year 2000 is nearly here
The year 1000 has nearly gone
Soon to be replaced by another one.

Eric Haines (10)
Hurstclough County Primary

MY HOLIDAY

We're sitting in the car and we're going very far,
We're going to the sea as a whole family,
A summer holiday is what we're going on,
Not a cloud in the sky and the sun shines on.

Children playing in the sea,
Making sandcastles one, two, three,
Stripy coloured deck chairs all in a row,
Sunburnt face all aglow.

Baby crying, mother buying,
Ice-cream melting, sand squelching,
People on lilos bobbing up and down,
Mostly making a funny frown like a clown.

Cheese sandwiches with some sand,
Lots of drinks in cans,
Mum's saying 'Wasps coming this way,'
Everyone starts running.

Vicky Barnett (10)
Lower Peover CE Primary School

BONFIRE PARTY

Bang, crash, boom, go the fireworks.
Sizzle, crackle, go the hot-dogs being cooked.
Munch, crunch, go the people eating the hot-dogs.
Shout, scream, whisper, go the people talking to each other.
Wow, cool, excellent, go the people watching the fireworks.
Splash, goes the water being put on the bonfire.
That was the end of the bonfire party.

Sarah Royle (10)
Lower Peover CE Primary School

CAST MY ROD

Cast my rod out to sea,
to see what I could catch for tea.
It could be big, it could be small,
but I would like to catch them all.
The fish will bite when it is ready,
so I must hold my rod so steady.
The fish has bitten and pulled the float,
so I must land it in the boat.
The fish I caught the name is Skate,
this is tasty upon my plate.
Sometimes fish are too small for me,
so I throw them back into the sea.
The small fish grow when put to sea
and then one day they come back for me.

Richard Roberts (9)
Lower Peover CE Primary School

SNOW

Snowballs flying through the air,
Big fat snowballs whoosh through your hair,
Plop go the snowballs right down your neck,
Oh heck.

Different shaped snowflakes big and small,
But they melt on the big warm floor,
Oh I love the snow,
I will be sorry to see it go.

Snowmen stand there,
And all they do is stare,
Snowmen shiver but we can't see,
But all we think is it a he or a she?

Lisa Barbera (10)
Lower Peover CE Primary School

SEASIDE

Waves crashing on the shore
battering against the harbour walls.
Rattling the shingle with a roar
drowning out the seagulls screeching calls.

Boats bobbing up and down
disappearing as if forever.
Enough to make the sailors frown
worrying if the ropes will sever.

Dazzling sun in the bright blue sky
a gentle breeze pushing surfboards out to sea.
Waves lapping the shore nearby
children laughing, playing trouble free.

Whatever the weather I go to the sea
the seaside is where I long to be.

Alexander McIntyre (9)
Lower Peover CE Primary School

SNOW

Snow is like clouds that fall to the ground,
Snow is a soft cushion on the grass, path and mud,
Snow is something to throw in balls,
Snow transforms the world,
Snow is something to think about,
Snow is silly, soft and squidgy,
Snow is there to cheer you up,
Snow is the cold thing on your car.

Carl Graham (10)
Lower Peover CE Primary School

MY LITTLE BROTHER BELIEVES

My little brother believes that teddies move in the night.
My little brother believes that the moon gives its own light.
My little brother believes that one day he'll cook his own meal.
My little brother believes in the Easter bunny.
My little brother believes that God makes money.
My little brother believes in the tooth fairy.
My little brother believes in Joseph and Mary.
My little brother believes in little Baby Jesus.
My little brother believes that he can never please us.
My little brother believes that television just switches on.
My little brother believes that on Sports Day - everyone wins.
My little brother believes it's very weird when he goes *Atchoo!*
My little brother believes that he's *Matthew.*

Leanne Barlow (10)
Lower Peover CE Primary School

SNOWFLAKE

S is for the snow that is white
N is for the noise that the children make
O is for ooow as they see the snow falling down
W is for weee as they slide on the slushy snow
F is for the flakes of snow falling down
L is for laughter throughout the playground
A is for aaah as they duck to dodge the snowballs
K is for kicking the snow around
E is for excited children smiling through their windows
S is for screaming and shouting as they throw snowballs.

Emma Hague (10)
Lower Peover CE Primary School

ELEGY - IN MEMORY OF GRANDAD PETER

My grandad died 3 years ago
When I was only 6 years old.
He will not see me grow
But my memories of him are pure gold.

My grandad Peter - my mother's dad
Was married to nan for 40 years.
We try to make sure that we're not sad
Because he would not want us to cry more tears.

He sometimes collected me from school,
And always brought me a Mars bar.
No one could ever think he was a fool,
To me he was a star.

He told us lots of stories
Of his days when he was at sea.
He visited lots of different countries,
Even some where they grow tea.

I will love him now and always,
He will never leave my mind.
He made us laugh with his little ways
But he was so loving and kind.

We know he is watching over us
But I wish he was still here.
He wouldn't want us to make a fuss,
Grandad Peter - we love you, no fear.

Frances Lowe (9)
Lower Peover CE Primary School

DREAM CAR

I saw my dream BMW last night
it shone beautifully in the light.
I paid £5000 for it
the price was too high by a bit.

I drove it off into the dark
then I heard a brown dog bark.
I ran over a nail which was a pain
then annoyingly it started to rain!

I pushed it to a car park,
then changed the tyre in the dark.
On my phone I got a call
'Come home - or no tea at all!'

I drove home as fast as I could
to be home at the time I should.
On the table I put my keys
then I started to eat my fish, chips and peas.

'I've got something to show to you
I've bought a car as good as new.'
My dad said 'How much did you pay for it?'
'I'll tell you after I've shown you it!'

Ben Washburn (10)
Lower Peover CE Primary School

MR SNOWFALL

Merry Christmas is the time of year where
Eating and playing brings you good cheer.
Ringing bells with a great big bang,
Rolling snowballs from my hand.
Yelling children in the snow.

Christmas carols high and low,
Heated house all cosy and warm.
Red robin singing in the mistletoe
Icy pond frozen up, with a crack down we go.
Stocking hanging in my house,
Toes wriggling by the fire.
My Christmas Day has nearly gone - but wait!
Angels fly by in the sky, past my windows flying high.
Sad children watching the snow melt.

Grace Hofton (10)
Lower Peover CE Primary School

BONFIRE NIGHT

B oom goes the fireworks
O n goes the wood - *crackle!*
N ever to be seen again
F ireworks whoosh, bang, ooh aah!
I nconsiderate fire *crackle crackle!*
R oar! It's towering flames, orange and red.
E xcited children running around
   g iggling all the time.

David Gabbott (10)
Lower Peover CE Primary School

MY GRANDMA

My grandma is very kind
My grandma is a very
good cook
My grandma gives me
orange squash
My grandma never needs
to look at her recipe book.

My grandma gives me
apple crumble
My grandma feeds me
crisps as a snack
My grandma gives me apple crumble
which makes my tummy rumble
My grandma lets me have my
favourite snack - chocolate cake.

Andrew Watmore (10)
Lower Peover CE Primary School

SHEHRAZADE

Thin and elegant
Light beams on her face.
Her golden hair shines
in the light.
Jewels make her face beautiful.
Her voice sounds soft, generous
and kind.
Her bright blue eyes sparkle
as she tells her stories.

Laura Boffey (9)
Rode Heath County Primary School

SHEHRAZADE

She looks as sweet as a sunflower
her hair flows gently in the wind.
Her soft voice echoing through the Sultan's palace
his black cloak lifts in the breeze.
Dark eyes camouflaged by his gruesome clothes.
He stands and listens
then his evil mind starts to plot.
Plots to kill.
But she is too clever for him.
She enchants him with a magic story.
Like never-ending words.
His eyes light up from dark to dawn
his power weakened when he hears
the sound of her sweet voice.

Michelle Sigley (10)
Rode Heath County Primary School

SHEHRAZADE

Soft and gently she creeps through the night
He strides up and down the corridors.
Wicked and powerful - he laughs to himself.
Shehrazade whispers stories like a summer's breeze.
The Sultan acting like a gentle creature.
Her hair like a wave crashing against the rocks.
Her clothes are the colour of the sunset,
As soft as silk material.
The Sultan's robes are a great island,
the colour of the blue ocean.
Not wanting to believe how enchanting
the stories are.

Lauren Holbrook (11)
Rode Heath County Primary School

SPRING POEM

The birds that sing all day long
sound like a person playing a flute.
The centre of a daffodil - orange like a ball of fire.
The thin fragile petal falls to the ground
and feels like a piece of silk.
Frogspawn is lying on the top of the water
as still as jelly.
The little buds on the trees turn out
to become medium pink blossoms.
The catkins are like little furry caterpillars.

Danielle Sharples (9)
Rode Heath County Primary School

HERE COME THE SNOWFLAKES

Surprising, strange, silent comes the snow.
Snowflakes falling down.
Winter's here everybody shivers, everyone will know.
Crunch, crunch, crunch as we walk down the path.
Pretty frosty and icy, hip hip hooray it's the snow!
They are all different - hard, white and bumpy.
All of them are frozen but they're still white.
Look out for them, they're everywhere.
But they are gay and bright.
Children play about and are always having fun
And afterwards go inside for a hot-cross bun.

Justine Bailey (8)
Rode Heath County Primary School

SPRING YOUTH

She brings out the daffodils
with their heads like golden trumpets.
The birds sing for her,
like a flute being played in the soft rays
of sunlight.
She plays with the lambs as they skip about
like little children.
The flowers bloom and the trees blossom
as she touches them.
She watches people doing their gardening,
glowing in the sun.
She withers under the heat of summer
when it's time for spring to go.

Aimee Townley (10)
Rode Heath County Primary School

OUTSIDE

I feel the wind brushing across my face.
Footsteps are lightly thumping on the concrete ground.
I'm wondering who my mum could be minding
in the Crèche today.
The still pond is shimmering with a light breeze.
I can smell the new signs of spring and see
the blooming flowers swaying in the winter's wind.
Orange wrappers are swiftly moving across
the damp playground.
The sound of heaters reminds me of
my warm cosy home.

Victoria Sutton (8)
Rode Heath County Primary School

THE SULTAN

The horrendous Sultan is like a huge volcano
erupting whenever he wants something.
The mad avaricious Sultan is like a giant apple
rolling around.
He knocks down anything in his way.
The fat, big-headed Sultan is like
swirling tornadoes going round and round.
His purple and black eyes watch
and flash with evil.
His dark green velvet cloak covers the world
like a black cloud.
Dead wives hover, haunting his castle.
His moustache is like a thistle
storming the Earth.

Heidi Banwell (10)
Rode Heath County Primary School

SPRINGTIME

The curtains part
the scene of spring has now arrived.
Tiny workers with wings make their wooden lodges.
The stars of the show are the big stripy bumblebees
bouncing around the stage.
In the orchestra pit, birds sing in harmony
with trumpet-like daffodils.
Miniature ladybirds appear from the under the stage
taking turns to piggy-back.
Soon heat will come and the show will be over.

Benjamin Woolley (10)
Rode Heath County Primary School

MY SENSE JOURNEY

The sweet sound of the birds chirping in the distance.
Cars rumbling past as I smell the fresh air around.
I see the dull sight of the grey sky surrounding the brown houses.
Water dripping from the drain.
A damp feeling crosses my mind as I watch the
infant children playing happily together.
Watching the still hopping frog to jump up.
Wind blowing my hair across my damp cold face,
Most objects are still and calm.
All is silent.

Kathryn Williamson (9)
Rode Heath County Primary School

THE SULTAN

His black evil gigantic cloak sways like sandy winds.
His dangerous phenomenal looking eyes disguised
in the black moonlight.
The violent glance of him is just like the lightning
striking the trees.
The majestic selfish smirk on his fat face
frightening like an unexploded volcano.
The evil black heart inside him
spells execution - like a tiger.

Andrew Cain (10)
Rode Heath County Primary School

FLOATING ASTRONAUTS

One big floating Astronaut
Flying in the sky like
A big fish
Like a snowy
White swan
Not black, but white as snow.
He looks scary
He's not!
Watch out - they'll not
Scare you as
Much as
Darkness.

Danielle Unwin (7)
Rode Heath County Primary School

SPRING

Rays of sunlight sneak through the clouds.
Sky suspiciously changes colour, grey to blue.
The daffodils are strangely trumpets.
The music drifts away like an orchestra.
New-born animals dance happily
As the grass sways.
Animals awaken out from hibernation
Enjoying their free spirit.
The spring music drifts away as summer draws nearer.

Hayley Baron (9)
Rode Heath County Primary School

SULTAN

The Sultan's evil eye looked down
His ominous face grinned as lightning struck
Rain fell
The waves crashed
The ground cracked
Mist drifted through the air
As the Sultan went into battle.

Nathan Meneghin (9)
Rode Heath County Primary School

THE ASTRONAUT

Big Astronaut, heavy and white
Flying in the sky like a flying plate.
White, spooky, silvery thing
Floats around
Reflecting in the sky
Like a swan.

Stacey Brearley (7)
Rode Heath County Primary School

MY AMAZING HOUSE

In my amazing house
The door is made of money.
The walls are made of snakes
There's a kitchen of flowers
There's a garden of hills.

Lianne Withnell (7)
Rode Heath County Primary School

SPRING THEATRE

Water ripples along grey rocks towards a stream
A silver flute with the sound of the birds.
Daffodils trumpet as they join.
Primroses sway as the audience examine the stage.
Roses of sun brings life like the lights.
Dancers prance freely just as the young lambs
Stagger to their feet.
Buds unfold as the curtains close.

Jade Griffin (10)
Rode Heath County Primary School

ASTRONAUTS

Big Astronauts floating around
As big as a swan
As green as a frog
As sad as a monkey
Spooky like a white ghost in the sky
As cold as a fat cat
As warm as a crab.

Sophie Newall (8)
Rode Heath County Primary School

THE ASTRONAUT

Cold white floating swan
Melting like a frog
Heavy, scary, like a black fish
Big Astronaut
Fat, warm, silver
Like a monkey.

Amy Merrett (8)
Rode Heath County Primary School

REASONS TO BE CHEERFUL

The things that make us cheerful are:

That there is no war going on,
Having a lie-in at the weekend.
When we are blue, we just ask someone
To tell us a joke or read some poetry.
When Christmas is just a few days away
We get butterflies in our stomach.
That my friends are only a phone call away.
Before we go on holiday we get all excited,
When our friends are out, our parents will
Give us help.
When we get no homework, we jump for joy.
That when there is nothing to do, we watch television.
When we watch a comedy film, we laugh.
When it's our birthday, we play with all the new stuff.
When our Dad's tell us jokes (even if they're not funny)
We can't help it - but we laugh.
When we go on a trip.

Jennifer Batty & Katie Hodgson (11)
St Basil's RC Primary School, Widnes

HAPPINESS IS . . .

Happiness is . . .
School holidays
Presents at Christmas
Birthday parties
Chocolate Easter eggs.

Happiness is . . .
Easter's hot cross buns
A day at the swimming baths
Going to a wedding
Playing with friends.

Happiness is . . .
A ride on a horse
Walking my dogs
A walk in the woods
Walking along the Canal.

Happiness is . . .
A big Christmas pud
A tasty Christmas dinner
A holiday in the Lake District
Eating a large toffee apple.

Emma Allen (11)
St Basil's RC Primary School, Widnes

THE BONFIRE

The fireworks dazzled in the night drawn sky.
Screaming and soaring - up on high.
They shot up and cascaded,
leaving their magnificent fury.
As they illuminate the colourful sky.

The treacle toffee melted like sticky sweets.
My friend full with excitement.
Listening to the fiery beat.
I put on my gloves, my head full of laughter
as my sister was frightened.
(What was the matter?)

The bonfire died
but its flames are still living.

Now the sparks disappeared into
its bed of ashes.

Daniel Bibby (10)
St Basil's RC Primary School, Widnes

CELEBRATE

Celebrate night and day
all the adults shout hooray.

You celebrate at Christmas,
Easter and birthdays.
We all celebrate for our school
holidays.

There's a special day for everyone.
Butties, drinks, dessert is a scone.

Everyone is having fun singing
and dancing in the sun.

Celebrating can be great
so come on in and celebrate.

Martin Roberts (10)
St Basil's RC Primary School, Widnes

PINK

Pink the colour of the balloon that drifts in the sky,
Pink the colour of the flower swaying in the wind
that swirls by.
Pink the colour of candyfloss on the stick
Pink the colour of the lollipop that you lick.

Pink the colour of the sky at sunset,
Pink the colour of the oyster caught in the fisherman's net.
Pink the colour of the gems hidden in rocks,
Pink the colour of a diary with a secret lock.

Adam Prince (10)
St Basil's RC Primary School, Widnes

AN AUTUMNAL DAY

Autumn is in November
it might be damp or cold.
The weather is very murky
there just might be snow on the road.

The sky might be full of mist,
rain coming down from the sky.
You might disappear in the smoke
and not go very high.

Leaves off the trees on the floor,
invisible wind in the sky.
The wind making you cold,
so go in a warm, warm house
like mine.

Rachael Fraser (10)
St Basil's RC Primary School, Widnes

PINK

Sarah's dress, pink and white,
Sarah's goggles, water fright.
Silky, gentle, calm and bright
My lovely pink in the night.

Pink clouds over the park,
Pink clouds in the dark.
It's burning bright, burning light,
Orange and yellow are not quite right.
It's better than cream, purple and blue
Pink is definitely better than you!

April McKenna (9)
St Basil's RC Primary School, Widnes

St Basil's Nativity Play

It's the season of Advent and everyone's
wondering where autumn went.
Snow is drifting from the sky
and decorations are hanging high.

In school the Christmas spirit is everywhere.
People giving cards to their friends and
wearing tinsel in their hair.
Excited children fighting for a part in
the Christmas pantomime.
Trying on their costume and practising
their line.

Angels walking in a row, their halos
slipping as they go.
Shepherds kneeling by a manger bed,
where Baby Jesus rests his head.

Sheep and other animals, watch with
delight, as Jesus was born on Christmas
Night.
The actors follow a cardboard star, as
they continue their journey from afar.
In the wooden stable Mary happily sits,
comforting her child as they watch
people feel a warm glow inside.

Parents watch with tears in their eyes,
as the cast of the production rise.
In the shadows the Head Teacher
stands, with a smile on his face,
clapping his hands.

Rachel Williams (11)
St Basil's RC Primary School, Widnes

SCHOOLTIME

Today is Monday, the first day of the week.
The children are all noisy but the naughty boy's half asleep.
The teacher is all grumpy and he'll stay grumpy for the
rest of the day.
If I didn't have to go to school I'd be calling
for someone to play.

Now is work time, the lesson is Maths.
The children are all tutting because
we're going to have a test.
Most got top marks, which is ten out of ten,
But oh! I've only got nine out of ten again.

Now it's playtime we all run outside,
Some play on the hopscotch and some play on the slide.
Some walk round with the teacher,
some ring the bell.
I hope I get first in the line today.

Now it's lunchtime we go and get our box.
Some people line up and wait for their lunch.
Some ask the dinner ladies what we're having for tea,
I hope we get burgers and beans - that's it for me.

Now it's home time we all get our coats,
Because it's raining, we all put on our hoods.
We all run outside and walk home with our mums,
but tomorrow's another school day,
so we do it all over again.

Laura Griffiths (8)
St Basil's RC Primary School, Widnes

When School Is Out

We all go home
and leave the school alone.
The pictures jump out,
and start to run about.
The alphabet jumps down
and starts to frown.
The cleaners are walking through the hall,
so they all jump back on the wall.
All the pictures jump back on the floor,
as the cleaners walk back through the door.

Mrs Tracey is still here,
and to the toilet door she gets near.
She hears the chain flush,
and goes in, in a rush.
To her surprise,
in front of her eyes.
She sees
A's and B's.
When she told everyone, they called her a fool,
that's why she had to leave our school.

Our old secretary is gone
and now we've got a new one.
Mrs Hodgson's her name
weird things still happen,
but nothings the same.
Our pictures popped off the wall,
and sneaked into the hall.
They got caught and were brought,
to the Headmaster's room.

The Headmaster thought it wasn't true,
and out of the blue,
he sacked her but she didn't care.
Now everyone wants to know
who the next secretary will be!

Emma Woods & Gemma Bellis (11)
St Basil's RC Primary School, Widnes

WATER WORLD

Water . . .

The great, blue heaven of the old rotting Atlantic
The depth of life, the golden key to God.
A source of fun and deep laughter.
The cool soothing luscious drink, we all rely on.

Water . . .

The powerful yet gentle Lord of the lands
The great resting place of the huge rusty
Titanic.
The undying liquid.

Water . . .

The blue mysterious underworld to great battleships
The Lord Poseidon's undersea terror.
The beasts of the sea call it their humble home.

Water . . .

Guards the ship of dreams.
It keeps intruders away from its secrets.
It is life itself.

Aaron Rose (10)
St Basil's RC Primary School, Widnes

REASONS TO BE CHEERFUL . . .

No homework for the weekend.
Reading a funny book.
Going to play football with friends.
Telling jokes to someone sad.
Having good news on Christmas Day.
Drawing cartoons of people.
Be happy for our families.
Friends who cheer us up.
Be happy to win the lottery.
Writing stories on the PC.
Be happy to score goals for the school.
Having a peaceful lie in.
Be happy to have a mum who looks after us.
Listening to music when we're bored.
Having a new baby in the family.
Being a part of God's family.

Mark Byrne & Leon Moran
St Basil's RC Primary School, Widnes

SILVER

Silver, like an Astronaut's suit in space
Like a silver baton in a relay race.
Like the silver stars floating by the silver moon,
And like a silver dish and a silver spoon.

Silver, like shining buttons on a brand new coat,
Like a silver castle surrounded by a silver moat.
Like a silver mirror with a silver reflection,
Like a silver shop with a silver clothes section.

Sarah Verity (10)
St Basil's RC Primary School, Widnes

REASONS TO BE CHEERFUL

I really like it on Christmas Day,
I get really excited when I go to my Nin's every day.
It's really good to hear good news,
And when I find out that Everton didn't lose.
My family are really kind to me,
But my favourite Uncle is Uncle Lee.
When I find out that there is no school
Me and my friends go to Widnes for a game of pool.
My Nin and Grandad are really special to me.
They even trust me with my own key.
To calm my little brother down, I read him a book.
He can't read - so he just looks.

(Nin is a nickname I give to my Nan).

Ryan Philbin (11)
St Basil's RC Primary School, Widnes

THE WALL

The wall stretches along the lane,
It stretches for miles and drives me insane.
There's not a break or a gate in sight,
And I've been walking half the night.
Just wait a minute, what do I see?
Is it a gate? Or is it just me?
I'll walk over and have a look,
It's still a wall, just my luck!

Emma Savage (10)
St Basil's RC Primary School, Widnes

LIGHTING UP THE SKY

As the bonfire flared
and the flames started to rise,
I could see excitement and laughter
in my friend's eyes.

Fireworks cascading in the sky above.
They illuminate and dazzle and give off sparks.
Leaving trails of colourful marks.

Children having so much fun,
with magnificent sparklers glittering so bright,
Bringing out colour on a winter's night.

Some people were frightened and covered
their ears.
While bangers and rockets were exploding
as the evening started closing.

As we tucked into treacle toffee and other sweets,
For safety, the ashes were sprinkled with water.
We went home, snuggled in our hats and gloves
and gloves with Mrs Jones' daughter.

Catherine Topping (11)
St Basil's RC Primary School, Widnes

PINK

Pink is the colour of a pig on a farm,
Pink is the colour of a warm, gentle arm,
Pink is vivid, cosy and warm,
I love pink because it makes me feel calm.

Pink is the colour of faces in a crowd,
Pink is the colour of a candyfloss cloud.
Pink is vivid, cosy and warm,
I love pink because it makes me feel calm.

Samantha Elwell (9)
St Basil's RC Primary School, Widnes

HALLOWE'EN

On my way home on Hallowe'en night,
a witch came behind me and gave me a fright.

She had scraggy hair and a big pointy nose.
She threw loads of spider's webs over my clothes.

I ran very fast and shouted my mum,
but no one could hear me
no one could come.

She pushed her broomstick into my back
I fell to the floor and heard my
knees' crack.

She said to me 'Little boy don't you be scared,
you'll taste nice with my lemon curd!'

I got up again and started to run,
my heart kept on beating just like a bass drum.

I started to panic and began to scream.
My mum woke me up,
thank God it was only a dream!

Scott Grady (11)
St Basil's RC Primary School, Widnes

HALOWE'EN NIGHT

On the thirty first of October
it's a very special night.
It's when lots of monsters and ghosts
come out to give you a fright.

Witches with warts
roaming around on their brooms.
Horrible green faces
invading your rooms.

Mummies and Martians up to no good
zombies and vampires
after your blood.

Gargoyles and Gremlins
running around.
Werewolves are howling.
Oh, what a sound!

Ghoulies and ghosties
going bump in the night.
All of these things
would give you a fright.

Devils and demons
quick on their feet.
Phew! Relax
It's only 'trick or treat'!

Leah Peeney (11)
St Basil's RC Primary School, Widnes

HALLOWE'EN

Knock, knock!
Who's there?
Open the door, if you dare.
'Trick or treat' the children say
A pumpkin lantern to light their way.
Witches, monsters, Freddy masks too.
They are all waiting . . . to frighten you!

John Poulson (10)
St Basil's RC Primary School, Widnes

THE WORLD IS IN A SARDINE TIN

The world is in a sardine tin,
All rusty with age.
The tight surroundings cram everything in,
Just like a tiny cage.

The air is all polluted,
No different from the sea,
All the fish are ill or dead,
Is that the way to be?

It used to be a pleasant place,
But that was in the past.
I think it should be thrown away,
But with care, it just might last.

Kelly Adams (11)
Sir John Offley CP School

HIDDEN EVIDENCE

Evidence, oh evidence,
I hate you, you stink,
I wish I could wash you away in the sink.
If only a minefield would explode you to bits,
Evidence, oh evidence,
You're giving me fits.

Evidence, oh evidence,
I wish you could go,
Away in the post so that nobody knows.
Evidence, oh evidence, if you don't go away,
I won't be here to see the next day.

Hannah McAteer (10)
Sir John Offley CP School

CONVERSATIONS

I'd love to talk to our Earth,
To hear of how much she hurts
When we dig for coal and drill for oil,
What is hers we steal.

I'd love to talk to the creatures in the sea,
To hear of how much they hate
Us dropping waste and polluting waters,
The world we spoil for them and ourselves.

Hannah Curwen (11)
Sir John Offley CP School

STOP

Stop chopping down our trees,
Stop killing bumblebees,
Stop squashing active ants,
Stop shooting elephants.

Stop polluting the seas,
Stop spoiling them please,
Look after our Earth,
For all we are worth.

Laura Lightfoot (10)
Sir John Offley CP School

COLOURED FEELINGS

Yellow is the sunlight of our hearts,
Red is the embarrassment in our cheeks,
Blue is the coldness of the wet winter days,
Green is the peace of being alone,
Black is when you are deeply depressed,
White is the calmness of our world.
Let's keep it that way,
Forever and a day.

Amy Stonier (11)
Sir John Offley CP School

THE YEAR 2000

The year 2000 is nearly here
It is coming in much less than a year
Come celebrate
Come celebrate
For the year 2000 is really near.

Michelle Bould (9)
St John's CE Primary School, Sandbach

CELEBRATION 2000

It's the year 2000,
Parties have just begun,
There is partying all
Around the world,
And everybody is having fun.
Music and bands are playing,
There are people everywhere,
Balloons and streamers
Are floating in the air.
The year 2000 is here
And here it is to stay,
Let's celebrate the year 2000
In any possible way.

Lucy Hill (9)
St John's CE Primary School, Sandbach

MILLENNIUM YEAR

M   ake a date it will be fun
I   n a thousand years there is only one
L   ots of people come to enjoy
L   et's have a party every girl and boy
E   ach of us will eat and drink
N   ew Year's Eve, let glasses chink
N   ever forgetting as we stay up late
I   t's Jesus' birth we celebrate
U   p to midnight, it will be late
M   ake it special, an important date.

Catherine Silvester (9)
St John's CE Primary School, Sandbach

CANDLE

A new life,
A twinkling baby,
A floating butterfly,
A flowering bud.
A dazzling star that shines on the world,
As white as a bride's dress.
A drifting cloud,
A happy memory.
One ghastly gust of wind;
A coiling twister,
A spiral staircase,
A cracked heart.
A sad memory,
At death's door.
The light that was once, is now no more.

Katie Harker (10)
St Werburgh's and St Columba's RC Primary School, Chester

THE WITCH

The witch comes flying by at night,
On her broomstick to give you a fright,
She has a cat that sits on her back,
Which has a coat so sleek and black.
She is so ugly her face is green,
She has a big nose and a smile that's mean,
She has a big, tall, pointed hat that sits on her head,
The sight of her could knock you dead.
If you're a good child do not fear,
The witch will never come near.

Mark Roddy (11)
St Wilfrid's RC Primary School, Northwich

A KILLER

Do you wonder when you play,
What your cat does every day?

Does it lie home all day long?
Does it go to school and get sums wrong?

No is the answer, and I'm quite sure,
They don't go and visit the cat next door.

It is very different in a way,
To what you think they do each day.

They creep around behind doors,
Then pull out guns with their paws.

They pull out knives at the double,
Then go looking for some trouble.

They sneak up close then *Bang! Bang! Dent!*
That's where next door's cat went.

Not holidaying on the coast of Devon,
But polishing its paws in heaven.

You may think this isn't true,
Because the owner of this cat is you.

David Mason (11)
St Wilfrid's RC Primary School, Northwich

SUNSET SEA

Amazing colours across the sky,
Birds soar and swoop as they fly.
Gold, silver, orange and pink,
Light the sky as the sun sinks.
The rays of colourful light,
Filter through to the oncoming night.

Waves beat across the sand,
Breaking white as they hit land.
The sea shimmers with magical shades,
A beautiful sight until the sun fades.
Birds soar and swoop as they fly,
Next to meet the morning sky.

Megan Renshaw (10)
St Wilfrid's RC Primary School, Northwich

THE LEAF!

A tiny leaf
Fell
Off my apple tree
Gently
Falling
From side to side
Softly, safely
Floating by.
It was
Just like
The leaf
Was
Falling
In a
Dream.
Then
The leaf
Slowly
Landed
On the
Grass.

Lyssa Crump (11)
St Wilfrid's RC Primary School, Northwich

THE MILLENNIUM BUG

The Millennium Bug is hard to see,
but it's here and there and in you and me.
It destroys computers everywhere,
Changing dates without a care.
Look out! Look out! it's near our home,
Mostly all at the Millennium Dome.
The Millennium Dome, its main base,
Living in computers without a trace.
The Millennium Bug causes lots of grief,
Even worse than British beef.
This outbreak is beyond prevention,
Tricking grannies out of their pension.
Truly, really this has to stop,
Scientists should definitely come out top.
Trap it, squash it, flush it away,
That's what most people are trying to say.
The Millennium Bug is nothing but trouble,
It's worth as much as 10p rubble.
The end of this poem is very near,
So I'm telling you before the end of this year,
If you come across the Millennium Bug,
Don't go hide, don't get a thug,
Takes these simple words from me -
Leave your computer and go and
Fleeeeeeeee!

Henry Chambers (10)
St Wilfrid's RC Primary School, Northwich

THE FOUR SEASONS

Spring
The winds are tough and strong,
Rain showers are frequent and long,
Baby lambs frolic in the fields,
Easter bunnies jump at our heels.

Summer
Summer is the time for me,
Long sunny days near the sea.
Having great fun all day long,
The sun is shining and the surf is strong.

Autumn
The golden leaves are falling,
The sunny days are shortening.
Squirrels are scurrying to and fro,
Into hibernation they must go.

Winter
The days are short and the air is cold,
Wrap up warm, we are told.
Christmas time is coming,
A time for giving and loving.

Ryan O'Connell (10)
St Wilfrid's RC Primary School, Northwich

THE SILLY CIRCUS

You can see the clown
In the circus every day.
When the band begins to play
See the clown fall down.
The crowd queues up to pay
While the elephants eat their hay,
And the parade goes through the town.
The acrobat starts to pray
That his tightrope won't fray,
And send him tumbling down.
The elephants are grey
In the merry month of May,
But the chimpanzees are brown.
The clowns bring tea on a tray,
But the chimps refuse to stay.
The ringmaster wears a frown,
But the crowd all shout
Hooray!

Jennifer Coop (10)
St Wilfrid's RC Primary School, Northwich

WELCOME IN THE MILLENNIUM

In this world you will see
People just like you and me.
In this world you will find
One love of peace in mankind.
In this world you will celebrate
With a giant birthday cake.
Coming through a dazzling proscenium
To welcome in a new . . . love of Christ!

Alexander Darwin (9)
St Wilfrid's RC Primary School, Northwich

UP THERE, UP THERE

Up there, up there in outer space,
Are there little men crawling around the place,
Are there big bright things, spinning round and round,
That have never touched the earth or ground?
Invisible people, moving trees,
Is there food like chocolate, bread and cheese?
Volcanoes splurting into the air,
Is there life, is there life right up there?

Up there, up there in another world,
Are there planets which have been whirled and twirled?
Music playing, which is nice to hear,
Are there football matches where people cheer?
Things that go *zoom*, things that *boom*,
Objects that whirl and twirl,
Little spaceships flying through the sky,
Up there, up there, so very high.

Lucy Parsons (11)
St Wilfrid's RC Primary School, Northwich

NIGHTFALL

The sun has set far away,
The joyful stars come out to play,
The night grows cold, the frost is keen
It crystallises until it is seen
And every blade of grass and flower,
Colder . . . colder by the hour,
The white faced moon casts down its beam,
Upon a twinkling village stream,
Which as the frosted night grows older,
The stream turns to ice, *colder ...colder.*

Sarah Boyle (10)
St Wilfrid's RC Primary School, Northwich

MILLENNIUM

The millennium year is very near,
So let's stay up late,
And celebrate,
You'll have fun and so will I,
After we will feel on top of the sky.

The shops are getting stocks,
While the women buy new frocks,
The men buy cars
And buy beer at bars.

The Millennium Dome
Is very round,
It's about two thousand metres
From the top to the ground.

Let's have a party,
And dress up all smarty,
Let's have a ball
And not dress up at all.

Let's put on our suits,
Helmets and boots,
Because it's the
Millennium.

Toby Cheung (9)
St Wilfrid's RC Primary School, Northwich

THE FAIRY

T he children took me out of a box and
     laid me next to a box of chocs.
H appy faces is what I saw, then all of a sudden
     a reindeer was plucked from a drawer.
     Then out of a box came some figures, then more, more,
                   and more.
E ventually I was put on the tree, like a new car for all to see,
     everyone was admiring me.

F rom all around I could see the Christmas dinner,
     and the crispy turkey,
     and the sparkling lights as shiny as can be.
A nd on a snowy night, a fat man in red came
     with a bulky sock full of toys and games.
     He left the presents under the tree and on them were
     my owners names.
I n a flash he left the room,
     without a *boom*,
     so no one would assume
R udolph led the slay
     and flew away,
     back home for a sleep, ready for the next Christmas day.
Y es it was fun up on the tree,
     but Christmas is over,
     they don't need me,
     they've taken me down,
     already!

Bret Ellis (11)
St Wilfrid's RC Primary School, Northwich

THE MILLENNIUM

It's the millennium soon I just can't wait,
Parties and celebrations, it's gonna be great.
We'll be looking back over two thousand years,
But sadly everything on the computer disappears.
We mustn't forget the anniversary of Jesus' birth,
He came down to save us here on earth.
The sign of this is the Millennium Dome,
It's the biggest in the world, so it'll feel like home.
It's the last year of the twentieth century,
So I hope you're doing all you can,
Helping your mum and dad, or visiting your nan,
So make the new year simply the best,
Make it loads better than all the rest.

Anna Ward (9)
St Wilfrid's RC Primary School, Northwich

MILLENNIUM

Millennium is a Christian celebration
It's 2,000 years since Christ's creation
London is the place to be, they're building a dome in
London's city.
Everyone is making plans
Not only in England, but all Christian lands
Now I don't know yet what I will do
It's up to mummy and daddy too.
Until the end of this century
Millennium is just a word to me!

Mark Swistek (9)
St Wilfrid's RC Primary School, Northwich

WHITE SUNDAY

It's fresh and clean,
It's pearl white,
The snow, the snow.

The boys and girls have
A snowball fight,
The snow, the snow.

It's cold and wet,
And slippery too,
The snow, the snow.

It's slippy and slushy,
Someone's fallen, *'Boo hoo'*
The snow, the snow.

The boys and girls go in for tea,
They've had enough, as you see,
The snow, *the snow!*

Shikha Chanda (10)
St Wilfrid's RC Primary School, Northwich

MY ROOM AT NIGHT

I lie in my bed watching the shadows go by.
I pull the covers over my head as I shiver with fright.
I feel I'm trapped in a cave.
No one can help me.
The darkness is all around me.
There is no escape.
When will it be morning.
When will there be light.

Simon Rawlings (10)
St Wilfrid's RC Primary School, Northwich

SPACE

The ground is dry like sand on a luxurious beach,
Craters big and small, deep and shallow, round and ragged,
With one side as light as the sun and the other dark as the night sky.

Moon houses have been built,
And the people have moved in
They take in the first glance of the morning moon,
Still as the stiffest statue, like a deserted island.

As it gets to late day the shining stars come out
The sun's rays die out and the moon glows like something unreal,
It's like a thousand glow worms shining in your face.

As the night comes near people on the moon need something to do
They don't have a TV so they amuse each other with board games,
Others will take a snooze so they are packed with energy for the next
day.

When it gets late and the people are asleep you can hear the wind
whistle.
You can hear the flow of the galaxy planet to planet,
You can hear the moon's rotation round the earth.

When the people rise in the morning, they go outside and have a
morning float.
They swim through the air relaxed and calm,
When they come down they like to have a game of golf,
They hit it high and it glides through the air hoping to go on forever.

The day for these people is great, they get all the fun,
Try to make your day just as good . . .

Christopher Hornby (9)
St Wilfrid's RC Primary School, Northwich

MILLENNIUM

What would I do for millennium 2000?

I would have a street party with all my family and friends,
But don't count on it, it will probably never end.

Maybe I'll have a fancy dress,
I'll dress as a clown with a smiley happiness.

Or I'll watch a spooky movie,
Or one that is quite groovy.

Maybe I'll have a barbecue,
I'll invite all my family and maybe you.

OK, I'll do all of them, I'll invite my family and friends,
And it will never end.

Katie Crofts (9)
Tarporley CE Primary School

WHAT IS AUTUMN?

Autumn is a time of leaves
Falling to the ground.
Leaves twizzle like ballerinas
Swirling round and round.
Autumn is a time of tractors
Rumbling through the fields.
With their turning wheels
Round with the ground.
Autumn is a time for dew
It falls on a spider's cobweb.
It looks like a fairy's cradle,
Which they slept in the night before.

Anna Threadgold (9)
Tarporley CE Primary School

MY FAMILY

My mother is a teacher,
She teaches all the time,
My father is computer mad,
He's away in London now,
My sister her name's Laura,
She's at high school now,
My other sister Emily,
She's really annoying,
I have a little hamster,
Who's called Sporty,
He is really naughty.
So now you've met my family,
I hope you liked them too.
My mum and dad like this poem,
What about you!

Victoria Stoker (9)
Tarporley CE Primary School

THE HYACINTH

Last week I brought a pot plant home, it's on my windowsill.
I wonder will it grow for me, my mother said it will.
It needs some sunshine, water too. I think I know just what to do.
Hyacinths are lovely plants, their growing keeps you in a trance.
First we see a small green shoot, that's fed by water from the root.
The leaves grow longer, now here's a flower, it seemed to bloom
within the hour.
The flower's quite heavy it needs a prop, a cane will hold it at the top.
It looks so lovely now it's grown, I'm proud I did it on my own.
I'll be so sad when it has gone, I think I'll grow another one.

Michael Cattell (10)
The Firs School

THE MAGIC BOX

If I was given a magic box I would put in lots of things,
I would put in the clean oceans,
Because it is nice to see the waves go up and down,
I would put in memories so it would
Remind me of happy moments.

I would put in the sunset,
Because it is pleasant to look at.
I would put in the wind,
Because it is nice to feel against your face.

I would put in trees,
Because they are nice to look at,
I would put in the birds,
Because they are nice to see when they fly around,
Those are the things I would put in my box.

Laura Dutton (10)
The Firs School

MY CHOCOLATE'S GONE

I look at it all,
It looks so yummy,
Even though it's bad for my tummy,
I say to the man, yes please mister,
But he hands it over, down to my sister.
I turn to her and gasp 'Oh please,
Don't be horrid, don't be a tease.'
But she eats it all herself, going 'Yum, yum,'
And then she sits back smiling, sucking her thumb.

William Russell (10)
The Firs School

The Land Of Make Believe

Lying in my bed at night,
Surrounded by an eerie sight,
Fairies dancing,
Witches chanting,
Pixies hopping upon my desk.

Pull down the covers,
What do I see,
But a doll combing her hair.
A flash of light,
What could it be?
An army of soldiers marching past me.
Then all at once, in the sky,
I see a horse flying by.

A goblin sobs beneath a flower,
Lost and alone.
Crouching beside him is a fairy,
Trying to comfort him.

A flash of magic,
What is it now?
My silly old bear's talking to me.
Flying by the ceiling in my room,
I see a witch upon her broom.
And from my bed I see my bear,
Rocking upon his wooden chair.

Suddenly, I open my eyes,
There are all my toys,
Just standing there.
Then I'm taken by surprise,
Was my pixie really sitting there?
And was my bear on the floor?
And fairy sitting by the door?
I suppose I'll never know.

Alicia Chatwin (11)
The Firs School

MRS SMITH

Oh Mrs Smith you do look pale,
And you seem so weak and frail,
Please come and teach us some history,
We will be good, my friends and me.

'Oh no my child, that cannot be,
For I am see-through, can't you see?'

'But Mrs Smith, that is not true,
You're a lady, aren't you?'

'I'm sorry my child, but I am dead,
Tell everyone that's what I've said!'

So I went downstairs and told the news-
Mrs Denton blew a fuse!
She said 'School's out, you may leave!'
Everyone drew a relieved heave!

Nobody came back for the rest of the week,
And Mrs Smith stayed small and meek.

Amelia Papadopoulos (10)
The Firs School

DAYDREAMING

Come on Dasha it's time to fly,
Up into the clouds of the bright blue sky.
'And the square root of nine is please?'
A thousand migrating geese.
On their way to a magic land,
With the sea by the golden sand.
'Queen Victoria died in nineteen hundred and one.'
Hold on a minute, is that a purple swan?
Guns go bang with daisies filling the air,
But Dasha and me keep riding, riding through the air.
'There were eight kings called George.'
The giant is looking for more people to gorge!
Dragons breathe fire right through their nose,
The beast was cursed by a single red rose.
'All right children, that's all for today.'
If I find the map to dreams,
I'm sure I'll find my way.

Lucy James (11)
The Firs School

MY MOGGY

My moggy has a cute brown face,
A wet, pink nose,
A fluffy brown coat with a
Thick black stripe and spots.
She has small white paws to run on.
She's a tabby named Molly.

My Molly is lazy,
But she likes to eat,
My Molly likes to stay inside,
But she goes outside when she wants to.

This pussy is fussy as
She doesn't like tuna,
My Molly does like a good old scratch,
She thinks the wall is a scratch-pole.
Miss Molly likes to run up and down the stairs,
Chasing after Polly.

Molly hates heights so terribly,
She kicks and squeals if you pick her up,
This pussy likes a snooze on my bed,
She'll ring her bell when she jumps up,
Miss moggy is a cutey when she sleeps

Philippa Kidson (10)
The Firs School

THE MAGIC BOX

From my box I would take out rain to feed the earth.
From my box I would take out the sun,
To give us light, day and night.
From my box I would bring out snow,
Because it's a pretty sight.
From my box I would bring out clean oceans
So the animals would have a pollution-free environment.
From my box I would take out clean land
So we could eat without worries and not get ill.
From my box I would bring out water,
Because we can't survive without it.
And last of all, I would take out of my box
Nice pictures to make me feel better when I'm sad.
That would make the world a better place.

Melissa Barritt (10)
The Firs School

PENGUINS

Penguins live in the Antarctic,
Ohhh, so very cold,
How do they stay warm you say,
Blubber's the answer.

Here's a penguin's life cycle.
The egg is laid.
Incubation by the male,
Blubber covers the egg.
Once the chick has hatched,
They gather together
To form a rookery.

In order of size,
They work their way outwards.
This keeps them warm,
Summer comes, they have brown feathers,
Once they fall off,
They show a coat full of colours,
New oily feathers,
For the very cold winter.

Louisa Button (11)
The Firs School

PLANTS

Pretty petals have a plant,
Shining in the sunlight,
The mighty stem holding it all up,
The roots so far underground,
The bulb the start of life.

Here it comes all the time,
Then it comes through, green on the ground.
It makes its stem, leaves and petals.

It's made it again, it's here for another year,
The flowers come so, so pretty,
Then one day it turns in to a seed,
And flies away.

Another year, lots of plants,
Everywhere,
The stem, the bulb, it's all there,
It's here for another year!

Robert Pierce (10)
The Firs School

GHOST AT SCHOOL

Mrs Burns the geography ghoul has come to
To haunt the Firs school.
She creeps around all day and night.
She gives the pupils an awful fright.
The teachers say she ate their books,
But that's not so bad,
Because she ate my friend's homework book.
Now he gets in trouble because he's always stuck,
Her class is empty she ate that too,
Except the pupils who are stuck by glue
And stuck to the floor by super glue.
We should go home and off she flew
And all was fine.
Except J2 who are stuck by glue and all
The other classes were fine but had no geography too.
The ghoul of the ghosts flew right away,
To her medieval castle, long, long away.

James Parry (10)
The Firs School

Dogs

They come in all sizes,
Big and small,
Short and tall,
Fat and thin,
Muddy paws when they come in.

They're always there for you,
Listen to you,
And answer back too.
They're warm, furry and nice,
Not like a piece of ice.

Some people call them Penelope or Jo,
others call them Jess or Mo,
Lots of different breeds,
Some English or Japanese.

Love them or hate them
Our canine friends,
Their love never ends.
Love long walks,
Even though they can't talk,
They make noises you recognise.

I love dogs,
They are live and alert,
Make noises when they are hurt.
They are not mute,
But are cuddly and cute,
Dogs, dogs, dogs.

Laura Hamilton (10)
The Firs School

TENNIS

Tennis is a fun game,
You can play it at night or day,
You have a ball and a racket too
So hit the ball and play.
People play all over the world,
They have a knock around,
So go today and give it a try,
It makes a smashing sound.

In tennis you run from side to side
Hit the ball then run,
So try it out, maybe today,
you can have lots of fun.
There are singles and doubles in tennis,
Both are lots of fun,
So play by yourself,
Or with someone else,
So go and play today.

Maybe I have persuaded you,
To go down to the courts,
To try it out yourself,
And maybe even play,
You never know, it might be
Your lucky day.

Sally Ashton (11)
The Firs School

EVENTING

Hurry up mum, we're going to be late.
'Not far to go now.'
'Thank goodness we're there.'
'Told you so.'
Quick, quick get ready,
'OK'
There goes the hooter, come on get going.
We're going to be last.
Over the water tray, over the logs,
How high are they, four feet, five maybe.
Down the hill, up the hill,
Canter, canter, gallop, gallop.
What's our time?
Yes, we're first! We're in to the final.
So here it goes again.
I am feeling great, happy, excited.
We've won again. I am so pleased.
It's time to go now,
But I've had a really good day.
Yes! I've won!

Melissa Ithell (11)
The Firs School

ALIENS

I have never seen an alien,
Because they're up there in Mars,
With a moon and lots of stars.

Some have spots,
Some have stripes,
Some have two heads,
And four windpipes.

Some have three legs,
Some have four toes,
How they got like that . . .
Nobody knows.

Now I hope you realise
How wonderful aliens are,
They may look scary,
Those wonderful things from afar.

Sarah Walker (10)
The Firs School

THE FOOTBALL MATCH

The players came on to the pitch,
The Manchester cool air filled the stands.
Some of the fans were clanging pots and pans.

On came Stam, Schmeichel and Cole,
The ref was already inspecting a hole,
With Ronaldo at home ill and the club with a terrible bill,
Inter Milan were pretty poor.

When the first United goal went in,
The fans were making a terrible din.
When the second goal went in
United were sure to win.

When the final whistle blew
Simeone lost his shoe.
When the Inter fans went home,
There was a terrible groan.

Rory Howard (11)
The Firs School

PETE

Pete is not a goldfish or a rabbit,
Nor a donkey, big and bonky,
He isn't a duck, nor a buck,
Not a hamster, small and furry,
Not a tree or a plant.

Pete is long and sticky,
Brown and small,
And very picky.
He hides very well,
In his food,
That's leaves and sticks,
Sometimes with prickles,
He lives in a container,
In my bedroom,
By the window,
Which is sometimes hot.

So now I'll tell you,
Who he is,
That's long and sticky,
Brown and small,
I'll reveal to you,
He's a stick insect.

Owen Burek (11)
The Firs School

THE HAUNTED SCHOOL

Arriving at school one day,
It was a very horrible type of day,
The wind was gusting in my face,
Children and teachers, there was no trace,
An icy chill went down my spine,
But I hoped everything would be fine.

Next in the distance I saw,
A ghost with a voice like a roar,
I stopped in my tracks and froze to the spot,
What I was doing I completely forgot.
I ran to the class and told the teacher,
She said 'I have never heard of such a creature.'

I started my lesson and tried to forget,
But the sight of the ghost I had no regret,
Then past the window I saw it again,
Was it my imagination, or was it the rain?

I asked to be excused to wash my hands,
To follow the ghost to see where it lands,
I saw it enter the technology room,
Then it vanished just like the moon,
Will anyone ever see it again?

Callum Rigby (10)
The Firs School

THE END OF SUMMER

The end of summer has begun,
The days are colder, leaves are rustling all around.
All the hedgehogs cuddle up tight
And when you go to bed mum turns off the light.
The days grow shorter, the nights grow long.
Wearing trousers, running around, falling over,
Touch the ground.
Plants are dying, so are leaves,
Many people wear sleeves,
Mouldy clover, whiter than the cliffs of Dover,
TV's on, curtains closed, roaring fires warm our toes
Lamp posts on, big moon bright, shooting stars are all the light.
Many people cuddle up tight,
It's time to say *night night.*

Jenny Simmons (10)
The Firs School

MY CAT

My cat I suppose is my best, best, friend.
I play with him every day.
He sleeps at the end of my bed each night.
They have fish fingers
For their yummy tea.
I love my cats,
Although they have fleas!

Rebecca Arnold (10)
The Firs School

MY KITE

Bobbing and soaring golden kite,
The wind is blowing,
My dear kite,
Swooping, diving, gliding,
Twisting high in the sky,
Landing on green grass.

Phillip Hopley (8)
Underwood West Junior School

MY KITE

My kite is yellow,
It is gliding in the blue sky,
The blue and yellow,
Look beautiful
It is gliding in the ghostly blue air,
And the clouds are shaped like cotton wool.

Aaron Pointon (9)
Underwood West Junior School

MY KITE

My kite is flying high
In the navy blue sky,
It is swooping so high,
I love it in the sky,
The colours are red, yellow, purple and blue,
It moves like a wiggly worm.

Amy Clynes (8)
Underwood West Junior School

KITES

Kites fly high
Into the sky
Kites can be
Shaped in anyway
Kites need wind
To fly high in
The sky
Colours of a
Kite will shine
So why not
Try to fly a kite
It moves like a
Fish swimming
Happily in
The sea.

James Dodd (8)
Underwood West Junior School

MY KITE

My kite is flying high,
The sky is deep blue,
My kite is a silvery moon,
A diamond eye,
It's sweeping, swooping,
Weaving, whooshing, banging, wailing,
Rainbow colours in the sky,
Up on the hill we're flying our kites,
Then it comes diving down to the ground.

Amy Jenkins (9)
Underwood West Junior School

MY KITE

Kite flying high
In the deep blue sky
Like a violet diamond
Blowing, sweeping so high.

Red, purple colours
It's crashing and bashing
Fighting and twisting
Diving, swooping in the sky.

Cotton wool clouds it passes
Like some paper drifting
Slipping out of your hands
Then it slowly lands.

Rachel Tweats (9)
Underwood West Junior School

THE KITE

My kite is swooping, crashing, bashing,
Flying so high,
Red, yellow and pink,
I cannot see it in the sky,
The wind has stopped,
My kite is falling down,
I try to get it up again,
It is like a plane crashing down,
It lands . . .
Bang.
I pick it up and take it home.

Adam Watson (8)
Underwood West Junior School

MY KITE

I was flying my kite
up in the sky.
My kite is yellow, blue
and violet,
Painted like a dragon.
My kite went up and up
and up into the sky.
I was good,
I like my kite.

Lee Stanley (8)
Underwood West Junior School

THE KITE

The kite flies high,
In the light blue sky
Twisting, turning, diving down,
Up in the sky,
Red, yellow and blue.

Joanne Evanson (8)
Underwood West Junior School

KITE

I'm floating in the sky,
Soaring high in the air,
Turning, twisting, circling round,
Like a bird,
Coloured like the rainbow.

Ashley Fleet (8)
Underwood West Junior School

MY KITE

Swooping and swirling there it goes
Flying high up in the sky so high
There the kite goes flying with all its colours
Red, yellow, blue and green
There it goes in the
Deep blue sky.

Jamie Buckley (9)
Underwood West Junior School

A KITE

My kite flying high in the deep blue sky,
Soaring high in the sky,
Purple, red, pink,
Soaring, diving, swooping,
And high enough to touch the sky.

Sarah Jane Wade (8)
Underwood West Junior School

A KITE

Kite soaring high in the deep blue sky,
Soaring on high in the navy blue sky,
It twists and turns with a golden flash,
As the sunshine splashes,
With a yellow speckled dash.

Dean Machin (9)
Underwood West Junior School

CELEBRATION 2000

The millennium is on its way
I am looking forward to that day
A new start, another day
The year 2000 is here to stay
The predictions of the experts say
We must prepare for a chaotic day.

Technology may suffer
And cause some unrest
Prepare for the worst
And hope for the best
To some of us
It will be a test
Just another day
For the rest.

Oliver Allen (10)
Weaver County Primary School

CELEBRATION 2000

The millennium is nearly here,
It's coming at the end of the year.
A time for celebration,
In every single nation.

On New Year's Day,
Some people will pray,
For world peace and joy,
To every little girl and boy.

Matthew Perry (11)
Weaver County Primary School

CELEBRATION 2000

The year 2000 is coming soon,
It is just at the end of this year
I cannot wait to see what changes it brings.
Here are a few ideas,
A hotel in space with orbiting rooms,
And maybe a house on the moon.
It sounds really fun for everyone,
We will even travel by balloon.
January 1st, I will step outside and take a ride to the riverside,
Sure enough close by,
The Millennium Dome will be standing high.
I will find out what's inside,
Restaurants, shows and songs, there will be something for
everyone to see.

Laura Sheldon (10)
Weaver County Primary School

MILLENNIUM

I need to buy some invitations,
We're having a millennium celebration,
I like the Millennium Dome,
But I'd rather stay at home,
I'll stay up late,
With my date,
I'll party through the night,
With the television blaring bright,
I hope you have a good millennium,
I will.

Kirsty Blow (11)
Weaver County Primary School

CELEBRATION 2000

M   y mother's got some great ideas
I   have a few myself
L   et's all decide how to party
L   eaving behind the 20th century
E   ntering the 21st.
N   ow here's a way to celebrate
N   ew Year's Eve
I   n fancy dress
U   pon my word that's great.
M   illennium here we come.

C   elebrations are well under way
E   ndless plans to make
L   ists of people to invite
E   veryone wants to come
B   uzzers, hooters and bells
R   ing in the new year
A   cross the world
T   he millennium has arrived
I   n every house and every street
O   ut of the houses everyone meets
N   ew Year's Day welcomes the millennium.

Anna Turton (11)
Weaver County Primary School

CELEBRATION 2000

The millennium will soon be here
At the start of next year.

Two thousand years have gone by
Since Jesus was condemned to die.

Much has happened in the past years
Hopes and dreams, worries and fears.

Deaths and diseases, battles and wars
Scientific inventions, government and laws.

Great books have been written, films directed
With technology now the world is connected.

In school, punishment was the cane
But nowadays there is no pain.

Now we've been to the Moon
Will Mars be next or Venus soon.

So now we celebrate and look to the future
The huge new Dome will be a great picture.

No more war, poverty or crime
Make this millennium a happy time.

Diane Evans (11)
Weaver County Primary School

MILLENNIUM ERA

Here it comes
All big and bold
2000 years since the story was told.

What a celebration it will be.
Tears shed in many eyes and
memories of past new years gone by.

Fireworks fizz, whiz, bang and boom.
Wondering what the millennium has in store,
Perhaps world peace and no more war?

People dancing, singing 'Auld Lang Syne'
No litter, no polluting but recycling for Mother Earth,
Keeping her well, giving her rebirth.

People toasting with champagne filled glasses.
Looking to the future to keep mankind.
Hoping a paradise we will find.

Whatever will happen.
Just look how lucky and far we've come.
To be born and grow and to pass through a millennium.

Daniel Astbury (10)
Weaver County Primary School

AD 3000

What will it be like in the year 3000?
I wonder if people will be living on the Earth?
Could there be aliens, pink with three eyes?
Will the stars be sparkling in the skies?

What will it be like in the year 3000?
Could electricity still power the world?
Will children be going to school?
Or maybe everyone will be brainless fools?

What will it be like in the year 3000?
Do you think the birds will continue to sing?
Will the air be so polluted they will have to wear masks?
Perhaps robots will govern and set millions of tasks?

What will it be like in the year 3000?
I hope there will be peace on Earth.
Will the crowds still roar at football?
Nobody knows the answers, nobody at all.

Anna Hufton (10)
Weaver County Primary School

MILLENNIUM FRED

There's a monster coming next December,
Who'll invade us all to a tether,
He'll get us in the party mood,
Make us scoff down loads of food.

The usual new year 31st,
Makes our party nerves shake and burst,
But this new year millennium bash,
Will make you run out in a dash.

The after affects of this monster are worse,
With drunken men roaming fit to burst,
The towns will be covered with half drunken bitter,
The streets will be lined with noise and litter.

You have been warned about this monster,
With head thumping music,
And clubs you can't enter.

I'll tell you a secret to keep in your head,
The name of this monster is . . .
        Millennium Fred!!!

Yazmin Harvey (10)
Weaver County Primary School

THE NIGHT OF THE MILLENNIUM

The year 2000 is a nearing
millions of people soon to be cheering
500,000 still in the night
waiting for the millennium to jump into flight.

The ball has dropped, the minute has come
Time to drink that bubbly and have some real fun
Pop those party poppers, glug that champagne down
everyone is having fun, not one tiny frown.

Stop the party, time to go, new year's resolutions to make
No more food and no more wine, not a bit of cake
all has gone quiet, not a whisper, not a sound
No one sober, everyone drunk, staggering about falling on the ground.

The day after the millennium resolutions made
People sleeping in their beds, waiting for headaches to fade
No more party, no more fun
lots of clearing up to be done.

Everything slow, nothing quicker than a turtle
'Everybody up,' shouts a neighbour, 'Way past sunrise' says
uncle Myrtle
The day is ending, sun starting to fall
Tomorrow is the time to clear away it all

Hope for the future, things to be done
All because the new year has just
begun.

Joseph Peter Reiser (11)
Weaver County Primary School

MILLENNIUM

What will it bring? Who is to know?
What shall we see? Where will we go?
So many things change, some bad and some good.
Is it worth knowing? I wish that I could!
I've seen just ten years of this century's change,
But I've learnt other things both interesting and strange!
In medicine and transport we've come very far.
Most people now own a computer and a car
Our homes are much better and so is our wealth.
The food that we eat, is it better for health?
To many of us the change is for the best.
But is it for all? That is the test!
Some people still know hardship, they're poor and they're ill.
Can we all change this? I hope that we will.
For change is worth nothing unless we can care.
Whatever else we learn we must learn to share.
An end to all war, to poverty and greed.
We have started to help, and we must succeed.
For Lord Jesus died, to show that we ought.
To care for all others, that's what he taught.
In 2000 years, since his birth we have known
Unbelievable changes but, we reap what we've sown.
Let's hope in 100 years' time we can look back and say
That we all changed for the better, starting millennium's first
day!

Mark Storey (10)
Weaver County Primary School

THE MILLENNIUM

My grandpa will have his seventy third birthday in the millennium.
In Greenwich, London the Millennium Dome is being built to
celebrate the year.
Lots of people may have their power cut off at the starting of the
millennium.
Lots of money is going into the building of the Millennium Dome.
Everywhere people will be celebrating the millennium.
Not everybody will be celebrating the millennium.
In the millennium I will have my thirteenth birthday.
Underneath the blanket of darkness millions of fireworks will light
the sky.

Many unpredicted things could happen over the millennium.

Thomas Cowap (11)
Weaver County Primary School

MILLENNIUM 2000

M   is for millennium and the changes of mankind.
I   is for intelligence and the power of our minds.
L   is for learning, laughter and love.
L   is for light which comes from above.
E   is for each of us for you and for me.
N   is for new life and what it should be.
N   is for neglecting the planet, that means you and me.
I   is for ideas, we each have our own.
U   is for understanding the planet, our home.
M   is for me and the things I have seen and playing my part to keep
our Earth green.

Megan Cadwallader (10)
Weaver County Primary School

PAST, PRESENT AND FUTURE 2000

This year people will be gathering from all over the country,
coming together for a party because they want to see 2000,
but did people celebrate other millenniums,
or millenniums to come?

One time back brings us to 1000AD
not a great deal happening but King Ethelred II was reigning,
who was not 'red'y for the Vikings which were going to attack!
Our people had got really mixed up Celts, Romans and Saxons.

Going another time back it was Jesus' birth,
but then only a few people celebrated it then,
just the shepherds, the wise men and Joseph and Mary,
but we know the story well because we celebrate it every year!

1000 years before Jesus' time, Solomon is around,
and it's Bronze Age in Britain.

2000 BC marks the bit between Stone and Bronze Ages,
Amen-Em-Hat II reigned over Egypt.

Another one back, 3000 years before Christ,
Noah's dad is around near the beginning of the Bible.

Back from there it's the beginning of the world,
just Adam and Eve, the only people alive!

But then there's the future, no-one knows what it holds,
they probably won't notice it with things like time travel,
but I'm sure they'll have time for a party or two!

James Richardson (11)
Weaver County Primary School

MILLENNIUM

We'll all wear silver suits
and stamp around in big boots.
We'll all travel in floating cars
and meet friends in space bars.
We'll have holidays in space
and take a hefty suitcase.
There will be scientists everywhere,
They will be working and we won't care.
Will this be good or will this be bad?
Will we be happy or will we be sad?
How will it be when the millennium comes?
Will we celebrate with beating drums?

Adam Ambrose (10)
Willow Wood Junior School

FUTURE IN MILLENNIUM

Happiness, celebration, millennium!
Balloons, fireworks, dancing, joy,
But I pause and think,
What will the future bring?
Technology, everything controlled by remote,
Everybody will touch the dust on the Moon,
Pluto will finally be reached,
We will breathe in pollution,
Cost of food will rise,
Computers in every house,
The future will bring what it wants!

Sirintiya Roberts (11)
Willow Wood Junior School

21ST CENTURY

Celebration,
A new creation,
2000 the new year to come.

Maybe solar power,
and maybe longer hours.
It's just the surprise waiting to come.

It'll be a whole new life,
and a brand new wife.
Everything's got to change.

Things might turn bad,
All scientists go mad.
A world of destruction and battle.

But just let's see,
It should be happy for me.
A future of anticipation.

Liam Owen (11)
Willow Wood Junior School

CELEBRATION 2000

People are happy throughout the nation
It's like a celebration station
But will life change?
And will it all feel strange?
Will there be camps on the Moon?
We're sure to all find out soon
So far my life's been great
But in this century
Will it all end up in a state?

Gemma Hancox (10)
Willow Wood Junior School

21st Century

Millennium, millennium
You will be here soon
A brand new millennium
Will we have camps on the Moon?
New year, new decade
Hope you will be here
New life, new century
Soon it will be your year.
What's in store?
What will there be?
What will I want in two thousand and three?
A future that's clean
A future with air
Not a future that's mean
But a future that cares.

Michael Hitchen (9)
Willow Wood Junior School

Millennium

M   y oh my it feels weird
I   wonder what it's going to be like?
L   ike it or not the millennium's here
L   ife might change, or will it?
E   verything will be different
N   ew decade, new life, it's sad
N   obody feels the same
I   feel scared
U   p from our bed, the old world's back
M   orning comes, nothing's changed!

Shelly Wright (9)
Willow Wood Junior School

THE CLOCK STRIKES 12

Big giant boots
Heavy machines
Lots of people in mean machines
Crashing and bashing, lots of noise
Masses of new Technic toys
For girls and boys
The new millennium exciting or what?
Waiting for the strike of the clock
Meeting friends in space cars
Eating new floating chocolate bars.

Craig Courtney (11)
Willow Wood Junior School

THE CAR

I got a new car today,
Will it start or will it not, or will it run away?
But I can't drive my car because it's just been stolen.

I phoned the police today,
I told them about my new, clean car
That's been taken away.
Will they find it or will they not, or will they just give up?

Two years later, 2001 . . .
The police phoned to say 'We found your car today'
I jumped in the air and laughed with joy,
I got my car back *hip hip hooray*,
I started it up, it just fell apart.
Was it worth the hassle?
No!

Christopher Roberts (11)
Woodfield CP School

LAWNMOWER

Will the lawnmower cut the grass?
I don't think so!
If the lawnmower hadn't been touched,
Will it cut? No!
If the piston went flying will it cut? No!
If it were repaired will it cut? No!
Only if I had the money, but do I? No!
If I weren't poor, will it cut? No!
If I had some grass, will it cut? No!
If I had some petrol, will it cut? No!
Will it ever cut? No, it won't!
I will use the scissors.

Michael Tyrrell (10)
Woodfield CP School

POLAR BEARS

Loves the water, eats the fish.
Has a silky coat.
Is it really clever?
Or is it really kind?
Why does a polar bear live in such a cold place?
Why is a polar bear white and not black?
Such a warm and friendly face.
Such big paws, but why?
Has a keen sense of smell, it's amazing!
Such small beady eyes, but why?

Claire Humphrey (11)
Woodfield CP School

GREAT!

Animals, are they cute and furry?
Do they love being petted and stroked?
Well some do and some don't.
Animals are great, soft and silky.
Cats are like big soft balls of fur.
Dogs are like noisy, long four-legged animals.
Hamsters sleep and just eat a lot.
Rabbits just jump up and down all day.
Some animals are slimy, old and ugly.
Do people love animals, or do they hate them?
I don't know, but I hope they love them.
Animals big and small are *great!*

Emma Finch (11)
Woodfield CP School

WOLF FISH

Why is it eating a crab?
Because it is hungry.
Is that all the teeth it has?
Not very many.
Where did it come from?
Where does it live?
What will I do if I get chased by it?
Swim very fast, I bet.
How big is it?

Luke Palumbo (11)
Woodfield CP School

MAYBE JUST MAYBE

Up in the trees monkeys swing
From feeble branch to branch.
How I adore the condor flying through the sky.
Gracefully gliding along the sea bed
The beautiful octopus goes by.
Up in the mountains family life lives on,
Mountain gorillas, beware.
In his desert burrow, happy but lonely,
The hamster sleeps away the day.
The orang-utan in the zoo dreams of home,
But fire burnt on.
Lions prowl in the long grass
Looking for grazing zebra.
Waiting female seahorse waits to see
How many babies her mate will give life to.
Elephants walk their last few steps,
They spot a Land Rover, deliberate fires
Drive them towards the guns, men.
Rhinos don't look too hopeful, young, just lost.
What will become, will they survive,
Will the animals of today thrive for the millennium?
Maybe, just maybe.

Mat Hughes (11)
Woodfield CP School

WHY?

Why are elephants so big,
And why are ants so small?
Why do birds have wings,
And why do fish have fins?
Why do cheetahs run so fast,
And why do snails move so slow?
All of these things I want to know.

Why do dogs bark,
And why do mice squeak?
Why do bears look cuddly,
And why do hedgehogs not?
All of these things I'd like to know.

Lauren Kozlowski (10)
Woodfield CP School

ANIMALS

Dogs are nice and sweet, they have a lot to eat,
Cats say meow, tigers just growl,
Elephants are big and strong, lizard's have long tongues,
Monkeys eat bananas, gorillas have hairy pyjamas,
Cheetahs are fast, snakes eat rats,
Cows say vowels, wolves howl,
Pandas are black and white, ostriches are tall for their height,
Camels have humps on their backs, horses eat a lot of grass,
kangaroos jump high, bulls can see red out of one eye,
Turtles go slow, flamingos fly low,
Koalas climb trees, giraffes eat leaves,
Sheep give wool, goats get full,
Parrots talk, bears walk,
Pigs are fat, lions build a habitat,
Penguins swim, hyenas sometimes win,
Zebras are striped, mice bite,
Bats are out at night, squirrels are out of sight,
Rabbits are scared, rhinos don't care,
Fishes have fins, deer have chins,
Frogs are black and green, chipmunks eat ice-cream,
Crocodiles are grey and green, hippos don't even like to be seen,
Dolphins are nice, whales sometimes are precise.

Stacey Ortega (10)
Woodfield CP School

NUDIBRANCH

What on earth is a nudibranch?
Is it a slug?
Or is it an alien?
To be honest I don't know.
Does it live in water?
Or does it live on the ground.
What does it eat?
It is all kinds of colours,
It is yellow, black and white.
Are there anymore?
I hope not.

Leanne Hunt (10)
Woodfield CP School

CRASH!

There was a strange glow in the sky,
At first a bit like a firefly.
From behind it a strange tail of fire,
Then an explosion as high as the sky.
Then a siren,
Shouting too.
From my window, I saw bodies,
A wreckage too.
Then it was over,
As it had begun . . .

James Tod (11)
Woodfield CP School

A Perfect Recipe For A Perfect Dumpyard

An old brown boot that's walked many miles,
An old, burst tyre on a battered, rusty car.
Burnt out fires and bin bags full of litter,
Watched out TVs on slept over mattresses,
Seagulls nesting in smelly, forgotten socks,
Some rotten, wasted food with some tarnished
Scrappy tins,
Granny's old slippers, worn out and binned.
Whisk these all together with a pinch of salt and pepper,
And there you have,
The perfect recipe for the perfect dumpyard.

Bethan Fryer (10)
Woodfield CP School

My Sporting Dream

Would it be possible for me to live without football?
Would it be possible for me to serve an ace?
Would it be possible for me to play for Liverpool?
Would it be possible for me to beat Colin Jackson for pace?
Would it be possible for me to overtake Hakkinen?
Would it be possible for me to row for Oxford in the boat race?
Would it be possible for me to outplay Tiger Woods?
Would it be possible for me to have a world-famous face?
Maybe . . . *just maybe!*

Sam Roberts (11)
Woodfield CP School

ANIMAL WORLD

Animals walk very proudly,
Tigers *roar* very loudly,
Monkeys swing from tree to tree,
Hyenas laugh, *he he he*,
Squirrels hide, bats glide,
Giraffes they eat leaves, I don't like buzzy bees,
Cats pounce, kangaroos bounce,
I think rat's eyes are like glass, I like cows because they eat grass,
I think koalas are cute, elephants play the flute *toot toot*,
Dogs bark, cheetahs dart,
Eagles watch for their prey, gnats live in the hay,
Dolphins speak, hawks have a sharp beak,
Flamingos walk, parrots talk,
Skunks smell, birds sound like a bell,
Badgers build a habitat, I wouldn't like to do that,
Snakes hiss, lion cubs kiss,
Owls sleep, frogs leap,
I bet the animals lives are *fun*,
Not when people come with a big rifle gun.

Charlotte Bell (10)
Woodfield CP School

CO-OPERATION

On my own I couldn't play snap or tennis.
On my own, a bike ride just isn't the same.
On my own, football isn't fun.
On my own, board games aren't good.
On my own, making robots is boring.
On my own, boxing isn't very good.
On my own, two player computer games are boring.

Warren Shickell (9)
Woodfield CP School

MY FRIEND AND I

Do you want to go and play in the park?
OK, let's go.
Do you want to share my crisps with me?
Can I have them all? OK then.
Throw the wrapper in the bin. No, I want to leave it on the floor.
You don't take care of the park, you should help and keep the park tidy.
Why should I?
Because you help other people by taking care of the park.
Oh well, I'm not Miss Perfect like you are.
I'm not perfect, on one's perfect.
I'm just telling you to throw your crisp wrapper in the bin.
No. Why should I? It's your packet of crisps.
Sorry, you're the one who wanted them all.
Who's the one that ate them - you, so put it in the bin.
No, I don't want to.
Fine then, don't.

You should always keep your properties clean,
Or anyone else's.
That's how you keep the world clean and tidy.

Habiba Begum (10)
Woodfield CP School

YEAR 2000

What will it be like in the year 2000?
Who will be there?
What will change?
Will it be exciting or will it be dull?
Will there be peace, or will there be war?
Will everything be here that was here before?
I guess I'll just have to wait!

Natalie Parrin (10)
Woodfield CP School

STARS

What are stars?
They are fireballs floating in the solar system.
How do they move?
Don't know!
What's the sun made of?
It's a fireball, but it's so old it's got bigger.
How does the sun move?
It doesn't, the earth moves.
How does the earth move?
I don't know,
I don't know everything do I?

Adam Murray (10)
Woodfield CP School

MY CAT PORTIA

We have a cat in our house,
Her name is Portia.
She sleeps on my dad's bed in the day.
She sits by the fire at night,
And watches the flames dance.
She sometimes bites,
But I know she's only playing.
My cat Portia.

Tom Knox (10)
Woodfield CP School

MILLENNIUM 2000

What will happen in the year 2000?
Will Liverpool win the Premier League?
Will Owen and Fowler be England's saviours at Euro 2000?
How will Man Utd fair without Schmeichel?
Will Schumacher be world champion again?
How many golds will England bring back from Sydney?
Could Charles become king?
Will Tony Blair still be there at number ten?
Will pounds become euros? How will we cope?
Will I be playing for Newton Athletic?
Will I like high school?
Will high school like me?
Where will I be in the year 2000?

Andrew Hamilton (10)
Woodfield CP School

HOW?

Why is the sky blue?
How does a plane fly?
How do birds cut through the sky as they fly?
How do cheetahs go so fast by?
How do kangaroos jump so high?
How come penguins can't fly?
How did humans come to exist?
How come we have to die?
All this, I want to know.

Alec Lilley (12)
Woodfield CP School

MY FISH FRED

My fish Fred swims so fast,
He is so fast, he is faster than my
Sister's fishes put together.
He eats very little, but is very fat.
He plays all day and sleeps all night.
My fish Fred,
I wouldn't swap him for all the money in the world,
He is my fish Fred, and he is not going anywhere.

Craig Ellis (11)
Woodfield CP School